40 More Great Flight Simulator Adventures

Charles Gulick

COMPUTE! Publications,Inc. **abc**

Part of ABC Consumer Magazines, Inc.
One of the ABC Publishing Companies

Greensboro, North Carolina

Printed in the United States of America

10 9 8 7 6 5 4 3

ISBN 0-87455-043-2

The author and publisher have made every effort in the preparation of this book to insure the accuracy of the information. However, the information in this book is sold without warranty, either express or implied. Neither the author nor COMPUTE! Publications, Inc., will be liable for any damages caused or alleged to be caused directly, indirectly, incidentally, or consequentially by the information in this book.

The opinions expressed in this book are solely those of the author and are not necessarily those of COMPUTE! Publications, Inc.

COMPUTE! Publications, Inc., Post Office Box 5406, Greensboro, NC 27403, (919) 275-9809, is part of ABC Consumer Magazines, Inc., one of the ABC Publishing Companies, and is not associated with any manufacturer of personal computers. Amiga is a trademark of Commodore-Amiga, Inc. Apple is a trademark of Apple Computer, Inc. Atari is a trademark of Atari Corporation. Commodore 64 is a trademark of Commodore Electronics Limited. IBM PC and PCjr are trademarks of International Business Machines, Inc.

Flight Simulator is produced by Microsoft Corporation and copyright 1984 by Bruce Artwick. *Flight Simulator II* is produced by SubLogic Corporation and copyright 1984 by Bruce Artwick.

Contents

Foreword / *Bruce Artwick* v
Preface vii
General Instructions xi

The Adventures 1
 1. Something of a Departure (Spanaway I) 3
 2. Upstairs Downstairs (Spanaway II) 11
3P. The Leading Ledge (Piper Only) 17
3C. The Relic (Cessna Only) 19
 4. Down with Rectitude (Spanaway III) 23
 5. Cutting Patterns (Spanaway IV) 29
 6. Finally (Spanaway V) 35
 7. Wrapping the Box (Spanaway VI) 39
 8. The Arrow 45
 9. Bull's-Eye 57
10. Time Warps 61
11. Hangin' Out 69
12. Waterline 71
13. Skoal! 77
14. Island Getaway (Tie-Down I) 89
15. Corner on JFK (Tie-Down II) 93
16. Gather by the River (Tie-Down III) 97
17. Fallout at Fallbrook 101
18. Ferry from Nantucket 103
19. Reconnaissance 107
20. The High and Mighty 113
21. Sentimental Journey 119
22. Lights Out 127
23. Sunday Driver 131
24. Tradewinds 137
25. Splendor in the Grass (The Manhattan Project I) 141
26. Reverse English (The Manhattan Project II) 149
27. Headin' Uptown (The Manhattan Project III) 159
28. The Easement (The Manhattan Project IV) 163
29. An Attraction of Opposites (The Manhattan Project V) 167

30. Landing Lights (The Manhattan Project VI) 171
31. Outposts 175
32. The Auburn Abstraction 181
33. Which Way Is Up? 183
34. A Fine Fleecing 187
35. Avionics Package 193
36. In Search of the Floating Bridges 197
37. Dawn Patrol 201
38. Red Quiver Valley 205
39. Thataway 209
40. Admire the Scenery 213

Appendix: Piper Area Charts 217

Foreword

Back in 1979, when I wrote the first *Flight Simulator* for the Apple II as a demonstration program for my 3-D graphics programs, I had no idea the project would go so far. Now, seven years, twenty-one versions, and a million copies later, the project goes on with no end in sight.

People often ask, "What is *Flight Simulator*'s appeal, and why is it so popular?" I think the answer lies in the depth of the real-world scenery and with flight simulator explorer pilots like Charles Gulick who find adventure in exploring the frontiers of this computerized "world."

It pleases, surprises, and occasionally embarrasses me to hear what these explorers find. There is a lot of painstakingly designed scenery in *Flight Simulator*, and I'm glad to see people visiting it. I recall designing pieces of this scenery and thinking, "I hope people manage to find this." The original *40 Great Flight Simulator Adventures* acted as a tour guide through much of this scenery, and *40 More Great Flight Simulator Adventures*, with its interesting scenarios and anecdotes, uncovers even more.

There are also a lot of bugs in the scenery (unavoidable with over a megabyte of database source files) that produce interesting visual results ranging from buildings popping up out of nowhere to pyramids floating in the sky. *40 Great Flight Simulator Adventures* and *40 More* lead you through many of these "undocumented features." When you see them, believe me, they weren't designed to work the way they do. I certainly don't advocate bugs in any program, but look at it this way— these bugs exist, and nobody (including myself) really knows everything that's out there. This truly is an adventurous frontier to be explored.

What does *Flight Simulator*'s future hold in store? While Charles Gulick and his crew of explorers (that's you as you fly along, in perfect formation, I assume) are uncovering scenery features, my staff and I at SubLogic Corporation are working to expand the world.

Two years ago we started Project USA and tried to digitize the whole country in fine detail. After completing Denver and Washington, D.C., we calculated that it would take us 1,000 scenery disks and 109 years to finish the rest of the country. Needless to say, we scaled back the detail, and improved our development tools. The result is the East and West *Scenery Disks*—two six-disk sets which include all major rivers, highways, cities, and larger airports. Although I'm not yet satisfied with the detail, 3,700 airports are a big improvement over 80. The limits we're running up against are those faced by any mapmaker. There is so much scenery out there, and it takes a long time to enter it.

I prefer dense scenery with lots of buildings and landmarks. We're currently working on *Star Scenery* disks that feature well-known areas in great detail. San Francisco is the first such area (and is included as the main flight area on the new, third-generation Macintosh, Atari 520ST, and Amiga *Flight Simulator*s). Tokyo to Osaka from our Japanese NEC 9801F version is our next *Star Scenery* area for U.S. *Flight Simulator*s. One limiting factor we're facing in international scenery design is the simulator's coordinate system. It was not designed to extend much outside the United States (astute *Flight Simulator* pilots may notice that the World War I Ace game, while supposedly in Europe, takes place about 250 miles north of Las Vegas in the middle of the Nevada desert). By using tricks such as reassigning coordinates to multiple areas, we're solving these coordinate grid problems, and we're always striving to maintain compatibility with all flight simulators in the field.

How long can this flight simulator project go on? Well, it looks like it's here to stay. Unlike many computer entertainment products, the new high performance computers will greatly enhance *Flight Simulator*. You can look forward to higher display speed, better resolution and color, and more features such as zoom and external view that allow you to watch your plane as you fly.

And as long as there are *Great Flight Simulator Adventures*, we'll keep opening new territory to be explored.

Bruce Artwick
February, 1986

Preface

Like its predecessor, *40 Great Flight Simulator Adventures*, the parameters and narratives in this book are designed to enhance your enjoyment of the remarkable *Flight Simulator* and *Flight Simulator II* programs. Designed by Bruce Artwick, these programs run on the IBM PC and PCjr, Commodore 64, Apple II series, and Atari 800, XL, and XE computers.

Though other flight simulations have appeared on the market, there is still, in my opinion, nothing to compare with Artwick's achievements in realism or challenge. The *Flight Simulator* is as close as you can come to piloting a real airplane, short of trekking to your local airport and signing up for flying instructions.

Listen to the Flight Instructor

This isn't a book simply to be *read*, but one to keep open across your knees or on your flight desk as you fly. In each adventure you'll find, among other things, advice, notes, suspense, mystery, and navigational tips. Reading about them will, frankly, be meaningless if you're not flying at the same time. Just think of the text in this book as the voice of your flight instructor, a guide intimately familiar with the local terrain and conditions, or just a friend along for the ride.

Don't expect to fly all adventures perfectly the first time, or even the fiftieth, even if you're a skilled simulator pilot. Taking the text and translating it into actual flight requires practice and familiarity with what's happening. Be patient.

More Than Mystery

This book adds a further dimension to simulator flying in that it offers specific flight instruction for ground maneuvering, taxiing, takeoff, climbing, cruising, "letting down" from altitude, flying airport patterns, landing, and more. The "Spanaway" adventures cover such things as power settings (rpms) and elevator trim adjustments to help you achieve precision control of your Cessna (Microsoft version) or Piper (SubLogic versions) aircraft. You'll learn when and how to rotate the aircraft on takeoff; how to set up standard climb and descent rates; when to start losing altitude as you approach your destination airport; how to understand and fly VOR radials; and precisely how to fly airport patterns and legs, from takeoff to touchdown.

But there's no shortage of the fun and mystery I hope you enjoyed in my first book, *40 Great Flight Simulator Adventures*. You'll fly with a strange copilot in "The Arrow," discover a weird world of mirrors in "Time Warps," lose your engine on takeoff, reconnoiter the WWI zone in your *unmodified* modern aircraft, learn how to slew anywhere (including around the world). You'll also be presented with a beautiful airstrip of your own in lower Manhattan, explore mystic shapes in "Outposts," closely examine the Clouds parameters, try to get yourself out of extended inverted flight, and much more.

Close, But Not Quite

Be advised, though, that the included flight instruction is intended purely for *Flight Simulator* and *Flight Simulator II*, and is certainly not intended as instruction for flying an actual aircraft. However, the principles involved are valid for real flying and are derived from those expounded in modern aviation literature. In this connection, the author acknowledges a special debt to *Positive Flying* (Macmillan, 1983) by Richard L. Taylor and William M. Guinther.

I also wish to thank COMPUTE! Books for its exemplary conduct in the production and follow-through on these books and the business of them, and editors Stephen Levy and Gregg Keizer for their fine cooperation and discerning contributions to the text.

Finally, all of us who fly *Flight Simulator* and *Flight Simulator II* are indebted to Bruce Artwick, the designer, for his great talent and the superb quality of his work. I thank him for many hundreds of hours of enjoyment, excitement, and challenge. Without his magical achievement, of course, these adventures could not be imagined.

The blue yonder is calling. Climb into the left seat, and let's get flying.

Charles Gulick
February, 1986

General
Instructions

Setting Up Adventure Modes

With the simulator loaded, press Esc (E on the Commodore 64) to enter the editor. At the top of the screen, under *Simulation Control*, you'll see *User mode*, and an arrow pointing to the mode you're currently in. It should be 0 if you just loaded the simulator. (If you're not in User mode 0, enter 0 now.)

Change the User mode number to the next available mode, starting with 10 and continuing to 24 (29 on the IBM). For instance, in the first adventure, "Something of a Departure," change the mode number to 10. Do this by entering a value of 100 plus the desired number—for mode 10, then, you'd type 110 and press the Return key. The User mode value will change to 10. Next, enter the parameters given for the adventure you're going to fly. The book assumes you're flying with Reality 0 and with landing gear down (the IBM Cessna has retractable gear, but we'll fly as if this weren't the case).

Change the parameters under the *Aircraft Position*—North Position, East Position, Altitude, and so on—as given at the start of each adventure. Do the same for those parameters under the *Environmental* heading. Change only the values listed at the beginning of each adventure. Leave Cloud Layers at 0 unless otherwise instructed. *Wind* in the book refers to Surface wind. Make sure to enter both the velocity (in knots), and the direction (degrees) of the wind. They're listed in that order. Winds aloft and shear altitudes remain as you find them, in preset mode 0.

Check what you've entered carefully. A mistake or omission can radically change an adventure.

Press the appropriate key (Ins on the IBM, S on Apple and Commodore 64, CTRL-S on the Atari) to save the given adventure's parameters in a separate custom mode. Until you turn off the computer, this mode is available. (See instructions below for saving modes permanently to disk.)

You can enter parameters for up to 15 (20 on the IBM) of this book's 40 custom modes while in the editor. If you want, then, you can enter a number of adventures' parameters before flying any of them. Of course, if you're in a hurry, just type in one or two, then go back to the others later.

Some Flying Tips

Before pressing Esc (E on the Commodore 64) to exit the editor, take a look at the first line or so of the adventure so you'll have an idea of what to expect. Use the Pause key (P) as often as you like to catch up with or anticipate the text.

Make a habit of checking the heading on your instrument panel, particularly as you exit to the editor to fly an adventure. The simulator almost routinely ignores the heading set up in the editor the first time out, and you won't see what you should, either on your panel or out the windshield. If the heading is not correct, reset the simulator by pressing PrtSc on the IBM, Del on the PCjr, = on the Atari, + on the Commodore 64, and SHIFT-+ on the Apple. Ignore a one-degree difference.

If you notice other disparities, such as the wrong altitude, reset until what you see agrees with what you're reading. After you've flown an adventure a few times, you'll know right away if something is wrong. If you continue to get incorrect results, recheck your editor parameters carefully.

Flying a Mode

After entering an adventure's parameters, exit the editor by pressing Esc (again, E on the Commodore 64). If you're switching from an old mode to a new one, just position the arrow opposite User mode and enter the new number. Press Return or Enter—you'll see the parameters change—and exit the editor. If you're using an Atari, you'll have to insert the *Scenery Disk* to fly most of the adventures.

Three cues are provided to help you follow the flight adventure events:

indicates where you're to take over the controls and fly the airplane. Don't touch the controls until then.

 calls your attention to a view you should observe out your windshield or on radar. (Note that colors described may vary depending on the computer and type of monitor or television set you're using.)

 signals that an action of some sort is required of you.

The 40 flight adventures in this book will take up three disks (two on the IBM). It's a good idea to enter and save to disk the parameters for all 40 flights in the book, placing the maximum number of flights on each disk (20 on each IBM disk, 15 for all other machines). Jot down the mode number and disk name next to each adventure title in the book so you can quickly return to any flight for another go. As described in the *Flight Simulator* and *Flight Simulator II* manuals, modes 0–9 are preset modes, leaving you User modes 10–24 (on the IBM, 10–29).

Resetting a Mode

While flying, you can always reset the current mode (in other words, start again) by pressing PrtSc on the IBM, Del on the PCjr, = on the Atari, + on the Commodore 64, and SHIFT-+ on the Apple. This is handy if you've lost your way while reading through the text, for instance.

Pressing these same keys while in the editor will also reset the mode to its original parameters. It's a good idea to do this every time you enter the editor to change modes, and necessary if you're saving the mode to disk. Otherwise, parameters will be those in effect when you entered the editor (when you entered the editor in midflight, for example) rather than those of startup.

Saving Modes to Disk

Enter the editor. Remove the *Flight Simulator* disk and insert a blank disk. It doesn't need to be formatted. Press the appropriate key (S for IBM; CTRL-Z for Commodore 64, Apple, or Atari) to save all the modes currently in memory. Once you see the *Mode Saved* message, or when your disk drive stops spinning, remove, label, and store the newly recorded disk until you need it. *Remember to use a write-protect tab for permanent protection—saving to disk destroys all previous material on that disk.*

Loading Your Custom Disk

Enter the editor. Remove the *Flight Simulator* disk and insert your custom disk. Press the appropriate key to load (L for IBM; CTRL-X for Commodore 64, Apple, and Atari). When you see the message *Modes Loaded* or when the drive stops spinning, remove your custom disk and reinsert the *Flight Simulator* disk. Press any key and proceed as usual.

Detailed Charts

For those of you flying the Cessna, we've reproduced the Piper versions of the four area charts and included them in this book. Take a look at the appendix. The four charts (New York/Boston, Chicago, Seattle, and Los Angeles) which accompany *Flight Simulator II* are far more detailed than those you find in *Flight Simulator*, especially where the smaller airports are concerned.

The Adventures

Something of a Departure
Spanaway I

North Position: 21203 *21216.5*
East Position: 6502 *6491.7*
Altitude: 427
Pitch: 0
Bank: 0
Heading: 205
Airspeed: 0
Throttle: 0

Rudder: 32767
Ailerons: 32767
Flaps: 0
Elevators: 32767
Time: 5:45
Season: 3—Summer
Wind: 4 Kts, 160

Note: For the most realism and, ultimately, the most precise control, I suggest that the Overcontrol Limiter *in the Piper editor be regularly set to a figure high enough to disable it. I arbitrarily use 80, which does the job. After a little practice, you'll develop your own internal overcontrol limiter, and how you fly as well as how things look out your windshield will be much smoother. Your controls will also function more like the Cessna version, so you'll be better able to make the transition between the versions.*

Because we're going to demand more precision of ourselves in this second book of adventures, the early chapters (those with Spanaway subtitles) are going to incorporate some standards. The airplane won't fly us; we'll fly it. Fly it by some specific numbers. Sharply. Like pros. Of course, if you're already an absolute expert at piloting the simulator, you can skip the Spanaway chapters. And of course, if you skip these chapters, I'll never speak to you again.

 This is Shady Acres Airport in Spanaway, Washington, a suburb of Tacoma. Make sure your heading when you exit the editor is within a degree or so of 205.

We're pulled up short of runway 16. I selected this airport because its strip is just 1800 feet long. If we can learn to do things correctly here, we can do them correctly anywhere.

Such as ready the airplane and ourselves properly for takeoff, taxi ahead, make our turn onto the active, continue our initial roll while steering smoothly to get lined up, apply back pressure at a specific airspeed to rotate, make a normal takeoff, climb out at the right airspeed and rate of climb, get to the correct altitude before we turn to our departure heading, level off with precision at our cruise altitude and speed, make minor adjustments if we weren't all that precise, and settle down like we know what we're doing.

We're going to do all that in this first adventure—all by the numbers and under precise control.

Tall order. But I believe you're up to it. So let's go.

Takeoff Preparation:
1. **Ten degrees flaps.**
2. **Two** *quick* **presses up elevator** (approximates takeoff trim).
3. **Check carb heat off.**
4. **Note altimeter reading** carefully, and mentally add 400 feet to it. You must climb to that altitude before making any turns.

Other: Where applicable, tune your NAV to get a VOR heading, call tower for weather/ runway info, and jot down wind knots/ degrees and any available destination data (elevation, probable runway considering wind direction, tower, or nearest tower frequency). If your memory's not the greatest, write down things such as your planned cruise altitude, and just as you make your turn to begin takeoff, record your time of departure.

This morning we're just going to fly locally, so there's no destination airport. We're going to practice takeoffs, learn important stuff about climbs, and discover how to make the transition to straight and level flight at cruise altitude.

You're now ready to taxi ahead, turn onto the runway, and take off. Here's the procedure.

Takeoff Procedure:
1. **Taxi ahead**, using these power settings:
   Cessna—1055 rpm
   Piper—850 rpm
2. **Turn onto active runway, still rolling,** and keep going.
3. **Steer to line up**, not worrying too much about the centerline as long as the runway is under you, and your nose is pointed toward the end of it. Follow the principle *steer slightly, neutralize, steer slightly, neutralize* for precise control.
4. **Add maximum power smoothly** when lined up.
5. **Steer additionally** if needed as you roll, following the *steer slightly, neutralize* principle.
6. **Rotate** when airspeed needle underlines the 60 in the Cessna, or reads 80 in the Piper. To do this:
   Cessna rotation—two *quick* presses of up elevator.
   Piper rotation—one press of up elevator.
7. You'll leave the ground.
8. **Dump flaps** when VSI (Vertical Speed Indicator) indicates a better than 500 feet per minute (fpm) climb (dump means take them off).

Climb-Out Procedure:
1. **Reduce power gradually to 2105 rpm** (Cessna), or **2050 rpm** (Piper).
2. **Trim elevator to climb at 500 fpm.** (Piper requires only one notch of down elevator to get this rate of climb, but takes a long time to settle down and then oscillates after that.)

Try to be trimmed by the time you reach approximately 1000 feet above ground level (AGL). That's not MSL (Mean Sea Level). Your altimeter always indicates your altitude above sea level, which is how airport elevations are measured, too.

Your airspeed will settle at about 105–108 KIAS (Knots Indicated Air Speed). In the Cessna, trim a notch at a time and watch your VSI. It will oscillate a bit before it settles on a new up or down indication. Try to anticipate its movement.

When you're climbing steady at 500 fpm, note your pitch attitude as depicted on the artificial horizon. Take a side view and look at your pitch in relation to the side horizon. With all these references, you could climb at 500 fpm even if some of them failed you, couldn't you?

After the sightseeing, I hope you're not quite at 2000 feet altitude, for that's where we'd like to level off for this demonstration.

To transition from 500 fpm climb to normal cruise:
1. **Climb to cruise altitude minus 20 feet** (approximately).
2. **Piper only: Trim nose down one notch** (in other words, press T, down elevator, once).
3. **Reduce power to 1905** (Cessna), or **1950** (Piper).
4. **Make no further trim adjustments.**

Your airspeed when straight and level at 2000 feet nominal will be about 105 KIAS in the Cessna and 120 KIAS in the Piper. The actual speed for the Cessna is higher than indicated by 5 to 10 knots, which you can check by entering the editor briefly. The Cessna airspeed indicator quite consistently errs on the low side. But you have to fly the instrument, not the editor.

You're now in normal cruise configuration and should be at about 2000 feet MSL. Your elevators are at what I'll call *operational neutral*. For the Cessna, this is 32767 in the editor, which is the power-up default parameter, and is true neutral. But for the Piper, operational neutral is 36863, not the power-up default. [From testing, it seems that *operational neutral* elevator on the Apple version of *Flight Simulator II* is 34815—Editor.] You cannot make the Piper fly straight and level with the default neutral elevator.

You can always check for operational neutral elevator, without referring to the editor, by doing this:

In the Cessna, operational neutral (and actual neutral) is when the elevator indicator is even with the center position mark, but at the lowest possible "even." In other words, if the indicator goes below absolute center with one additional notch of down elevator, then you were at operational neutral before you added that notch.

In the Piper, operational neutral (but not editor neutral) is when the elevator indicator is sitting just atop the center position mark, but at the highest possible position which will preserve that indication. In other words, if the indicator moves up from its neutral position with one additional notch of up elevator, then you were at operational neutral before you added that notch.

Operational neutral is important in our kind of precision flying, because once you're there, and know you're there, everything gets easier, as the examples in forthcoming Spanaway adventures will show.

Use this standard takeoff/departure procedure on all your flights so that it becomes a habit. If your cruise altitude is higher, you may need a higher power setting to stay straight and level when you get up there. So use a higher power setting. But don't switch from the trim settings covered above unless and until you can't achieve the desired result with power.

As you'll no doubt gather from these suggested procedures, it's entirely possible, and very useful, to empirically establish specific rpms for specific flight levels and keep a list of these rpms. Nowhere will your elevators be displaced from neutral by more than one notch.

Now do a 180 to the left to bring your aircraft to a heading around 340, and go back and shoot a landing at Shady Acres. You'll see three airports pop out of the landscape as you fly. Shady Acres is the middle one. You'll be more or less downwind for runway 16, so you'll land opposite the direction you're flying. Make a note of how well or poorly you do, because a little further on in this book you'll probably see a vast improvement in your landings as well as all your other procedures.

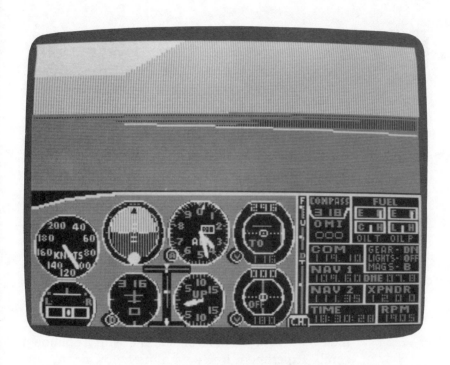

Upstairs
Downstairs
Spanaway II

North Position: 20941
East Position: 6395
Altitude: 2200
Pitch: 0 (IBM only)
Pitch: 359 (all except IBM)
Bank: 0
Heading: 280
Airspeed: 115 (IBM only)
Airspeed: 120 (all except IBM)
Throttle: 20479 (IBM only)

Throttle: 20480 (all except IBM)
Rudder: 32767
Ailerons: 32767
Flaps: 0
Elevators: 32767 (IBM)
Elevators: 34815 (Apple)
Elevators: 36863 (64 and Atari)
Time: 18:00
Season: 3—Summer
Wind: 4 Kts, 160

You're inbound for Spanaway Airport (not Shady Acres, where we took off in the previous adventure, and which is also in the city of Spanaway). Let's learn some new precision control techniques in flight.

Tune your NAV to McChord OMNI, 109.6, which is only a couple of miles from Spanaway Airport. Your DME will show you how far out you are. Center the OBI needle to fly TO the station, and get on that heading.

Important: When you bank the airplane more than a few degrees, give one notch of up elevator to maintain your altitude. Then take off the notch as you level your wings.

While enroute, we're going to explore a superior method of altitude control, starting with a shallow climb. Experiment freely with the following procedures.

> **To climb 250 fpm from normal straight/level cruise:**
> 1. **Increase power by 100 rpm.**
> 2. **At target altitude, decrease power by same amount.**
> 3. **Make no elevator trim or additional power adjustments** unless and until needed due to higher altitude.

The 250 fpm climb is useful when you want to make a small adjustment upward in altitude. Note that airspeed remains virtually constant. And though the Piper in particular, hunts and pecks quite a while to figure out what it's supposed to be doing, the use of power, rather than back pressure on the yoke, provides a far greater degree of precision and much less wallowing around. If you need proof of this while flying the Piper, get straight and level and—looking out your left or right side—give one notch of up elevator. Note the violent changes in attitude. See how they register in wild swings of your VSI. And watch your airspeed indicator make like a pendulum until your VSI finally settles on about 250 fpm up. The same thing happens in the opposite direction when you take off the notch of elevator you added. These contortions are not nearly as pronounced in the Cessna, but power in both cases provides far more precise control.

The point is that the aircraft will pitch naturally as a result of the power applied—*pitch follows power.* Think of the throttle as your altitude control. Let's demonstrate this a few more ways.

> **To climb 500 fpm from normal straight/level cruise:**
> 1. **Increase power by 200 rpm (Cessna), or 300 rpm (Piper).**
> 2. **At target altitude, decrease power by same amount.**
> 3. **Make no elevator trim or further power adjustments** unless and until needed due to higher altitude.

Again, airspeed remains virtually constant, and climb, once established, is very stable.

> **To descend 250 fpm from normal straight/level cruise:**
> 1. **Reduce power by 100 rpm (Cessna), or one notch (Piper).** (Piper rpms vary while descending.)

> 2. **At target altitude, increase power by same amount.**
> 3. **Make no elevator trim or further power adjustments** unless and until needed due to lower altitude.

> **To descend 500 fpm from normal straight/level cruise:**
> 1. **Reduce power by 200 rpm (Cessna), or three notches (Piper).**
> 2. **At target altitude, increase power by same amount.**
> 3. **Make no elevator trim or further power adjustments** unless and until needed due to lower altitude.

Try the altitude adjustments described above a number of times until you feel comfortable with them. Try getting the same results with elevator trim adjustments, and decide for yourself which you like better—altitude control with pitch, with power, or with pitch plus power. If you wind up liking power best, with pitch changes only where a specific power setting won't yield the desired vertical speed or hold a specific altitude, welcome to the group. It includes a lot of pilots. (But then, so does the other philosophy. At least now you *have* a philosophy, whether or not it embodies something called *Absolute Truth*.)

After you've practiced these ascents and descents, continue your flight to Spanaway if you like, or move right on to the next adventure.

In the next Spanaway adventures, we'll see how power works equally well in transitioning to pattern altitude; then we'll take a look at airspeed and how to control it deftly. But before we do that, we'll take a little detour around two strange phenomena, one visible from only the Piper and the other only from the Cessna. Don't worry—no one is cheated—everyone winds up with 40 adventures.

The Leading Ledge
Piper Only

North Position: 21000	**Rudder:** 32767
East Position: 6429	**Ailerons:** 32767
Altitude: 4000	**Flaps:** 0
Pitch: 0	**Elevators:** 36863 (64 and Atari)
Bank: 0	**Elevators:** 34815 (Apple only)
Heading: 350	**Time:** 15:00
Airspeed: 126	**Season:** 3—Summer
Throttle: 22527	**Wind:** 4 Kts, 160

 You're about 34 miles from Spanaway Airport, and all set to pick up a heading to McChord OMNI. But then you glance off to your right and see a weird-looking object. Just have to fly over and see what that thing is—a crashed aircraft, fallen-down skyscraper, chip off the old block?

When this mysterious object is straight ahead out your windscreen, pause to look at it a bit. It looks like an inclined runway, with a snow bank at the end of it, or a ledge that drops off rather abruptly to punish those who don't get airborne quickly enough. (In the Apple version, you won't see anything remotely resembling a snowbank.) If it's a mountain, it sure has an odd shape.

Unpause and continue flying straight toward it.

No, no! I said fly straight toward it. Hey! Fly toward it!

Where'd that thing go, anyway? And what was
it, or is it?

My guess is that it was—or is—a hole Bruce
Artwick tore in his orthogonal coordinate grid
overlaid on his Lambert Conformal Conic Projection. Maybe one day in frustration....

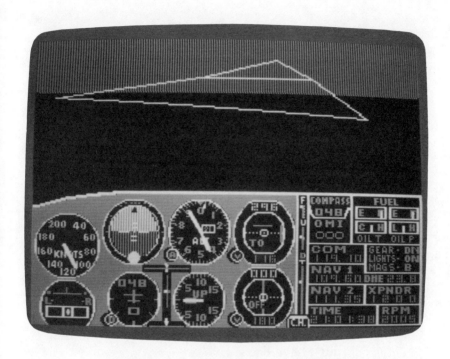

The Relic
Cessna Only

North Position: 21070
East Position: 6511
Altitude: 3900
Pitch: 0
Bank: 0
Heading: 49
Airspeed: 120
Throttle: 22527

Rudder: 32767
Ailerons: 32767
Flaps: 0
Elevators: 32767
Time: 21:00
Season: 3—Summer
Wind: 5 Kts, 230

You can fly this hands off if you like.

What's ahead is a rather antique curio. It's what's left of the framework of a house that blew down in a tornado in the 1930s. Kind of bleak on the landscape at dusk, hmmm?

Or maybe it was a tornado in the 1920s. Or a hurricane. Or maybe a fire.

Seems like it's so close, yet we fly quite awhile and don't seem to come up on it very fast.

Might be fun to fly right through the frame. Looks like we have plenty of room. Looks like we can fly right through it and into the horizon.

Carumba! What a big house it must have been. And almost flattened. Some kind of wind that must have been.

Everything seems fine for a fly-through. Looks like we'll pass right through the main structure, underneath the attic floor and just below the peak. Kind of weird. Like making some kind of ghostly pass through a skeleton.

Roof reaches way up into the sky.

Well, nothing in our way. If we had a skyhook, we could probably swing from that rafter that crosses below the peak.

Such a slender structure to stand all these years. Looks like a breeze could blow it over.

And when the last beam of the roof slips away from view, there's just the horizon and the dark earth below.

But think of it. We didn't fly through this relic in some strange state of slow motion. We went through it at a hundred miles an hour or more. Couple of miles a minute. And look at our altitude. How wide must such a house have been? How high?

What kind of creature leaves a skeleton like that?

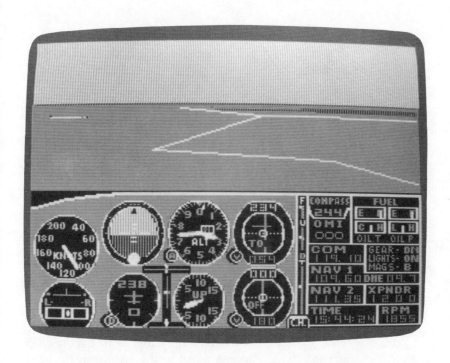

Down with Rectitude

Spanaway III

North Position: 21183
East Position: 6733
Altitude: 4000
Pitch: 0
Bank: 0
Heading: 339
Airspeed: 120 (IBM only)
Airspeed: 126 (all except IBM)
Throttle: 22527

Rudder: 32767
Ailerons: 32767
Flaps: 0
Elevators: 32767 (IBM)
Elevators: 34185 (Apple)
Elevators: 36863 (64 and Atari)
Time: 15:30
Season: 3—Summer
Wind: 0 Kts, 0

Note: Use Pause frequently during this adventure, and regularly read ahead so that you know when to do what.

Time now to tune McChord OMNI on 109.6 and get a heading to the vicinity of Spanaway Airport. Center the OBI needle, then turn smartly to the heading indicated. Your course will probably be somewhere in the vicinity of 225 to 245, but as long as the needle's centered, that's the radial you want to fly.

You should be straight and level at 4000 feet, so if you're not, it's time to get that way.

Very soon, you'll be able to see some of the southern portion of Puget Sound ahead. The highways swinging in from the north are Interstates 5 and 405. Just south of where they merge to become I-5 is the city of Tacoma. And at the southern tip of Tacoma is our destination airport, Spanaway. Elevation 385 feet.

Note your rpm reading. This is the power setting it takes to cruise straight and level—with elevator at operational neutral—at the altitude you're flying. (Your aircraft may not hold its altitude exactly; you'll have to add 100 rpm occasionally—use 50 rpm in the Cessna—then reduce by that much again.)

Now we'll try an experiment.

Make just this single control change—reduce your power to 1905 if you're flying the Cessna, or in the case of the Piper, reduce power two notches. Don't make any elevator/trim adjustments. You'll soon find yourself descending at 250 to 300 feet per minute. In your instrument scan, pay special attention to your altimeter and your vertical speed indicator. Note that as your altitude decreases, so does your rate of descent. While you go from 4000 to 3000 feet, your rate of descent drops from 300 to considerably less than that. And as the descent continues, the VSI indicates an ever shallower rate. Will this go on indefinitely until the VSI reaches zero? Yes.

Then, still with the same settings, will the aircraft start to climb? No.

Remember the *operationally neutral* elevator setting (and forget the fact that you're overflying McChord, and Spanaway, too, in this demonstration. What we're learning here is important, and we'll go back and fly home shortly). Continue straight ahead until your VSI, other instruments, and out-the-side views indicate you're straight and level. It takes a while because your rate of descent gets ever slighter as your altitude bleeds off. Somewhere in the general vicinity of 2300 to 2500 feet you'll stop descending. And you won't start climbing.

Here's more proof that *pitch follows power.* (And it's worthwhile noting that your airspeed has varied little more than a hair all the while.)

If pitch follows power, it follows that we can increase our pitch (up or down, but in this case down) to whatever we want simply by increasing or decreasing power setting. And by the same token, we can precisely control our rate of descent or climb to match any objective—such as getting to pattern altitude in a given number of minutes— by varying power only. *Because our procedure keeps airspeed constant.*

As soon as you're satisfied that the airplane flies straight and level when you combine a specific rpm with operationally neutral elevator/trim, you'll be ready to go to the next paragraph. There we'll learn how to "let down" from a given altitude in a given number of minutes to put ourselves at or near pattern altitude for our destination.

Restart this flight. Your NAV is already tuned to McChord OMNI, and you're probably around 30 to 40 miles from the station. Center the OBI needle and turn to the exact heading for McChord as soon as you can.

Consider this: You're at approximately 4000 feet. Spanaway's elevation is 385 feet. Pattern altitude there (or at any airport, unless advised otherwise) is 800 to 1000 feet above ground level. In the case of Spanaway, that means pattern altitude is somewhere between 1185 and 1385 feet. For our present purposes, let's say 1400. That's your target altitude—the altitude you want when you enter the traffic pattern at Spanaway.

So a bit of brilliant mathematics (4000 minus 1400) tells you you'll want to lose 2600 feet somewhere between here and Spanaway. Fine. But you don't want to lose it just any way and just any time. We're being *precise* around here.

Part of being precise is that we'll *always* (or normally, at the very least) use a descent rate of 500 feet per minute when descending from cruise altitude to pattern altitude enroute to a landing.

This means we need two minutes to lose a thousand feet. That gives us the formula
$$T = A \times 2$$
where T is time in minutes and A is altitude

change required in thousands of feet. Thus, it will take about 5.2 minutes to lose 2600 feet of altitude (2.6 × 2 = 5.2). Note that the same formula works for altitude gain as well, so long as our VSI reads 500.

For making quick mental calculations, we can figure our aircraft travels about two nautical miles per minute. Multiplying the minutes we need for the desired altitude change by two gives us the distance we need for making the change. The formula is thus

D = T × 2

where D is distance required and T is time in minutes. It will require about 10.4 miles to lose the 2600 feet of altitude.

Unfortunately, we never fly an absolute straight line, either horizontally or vertically, and it takes time to transition from straight and level to 500 fpm down (or up). Add to that the fact that we want time to get into pattern airspeed *before* we get into the pattern. So it's best to be on the conservative side when using these formulas. We also have to consider the wind strength and direction, probable variations in airspeed, instrument error, and such. Clocking your flight for a minute while checking the distance traveled on your DME will give you as accurate an estimate of your groundspeed as you're going to get, and that's a reasonable figure to use. But don't be dismayed if you're a minute or so off in your timing and a few hundred feet or more off your altitude. The formulas are simply aids to calculations that you'll make while you fly. What you see out your windshield and what you have to do as you come up on your destination are all factors in the last phase—and every phase—of your flight.

By the way, another formula for start-descent distance, one without reference to time, is

SD = A × 4

where *SD* is start-descent distance, and *A* is the altitude (in thousands of feet) that you need to lose. This formula assumes that at 120 knots, you'll travel four nautical miles in the two minutes it takes to descend 1000 feet.

If the DME signal, which radiates from the VOR station, is not precisely at our destination, simply interpolate a bit, using your chart and precision measuring equipment like a thumb or a pencil eraser. (Here again, the lack of detailed charts in the Microsoft version becomes apparent—if you're flying the Cessna, I highly recommend that you get yourself some FAA sectional charts.)

With all this information, go ahead and plan your letdown for Spanaway. But as soon as your VSI indicates a steady 500 fpm descent, *exit to the editor*. If this is your first flight in the present adventure, type the number 114 to set up the *existing* in-flight parameters as User mode 14 (or use any available mode you wish if you're not storing these adventures in sequence). Save the mode. Then you'll be able to return to this moment of this flight and refly it.

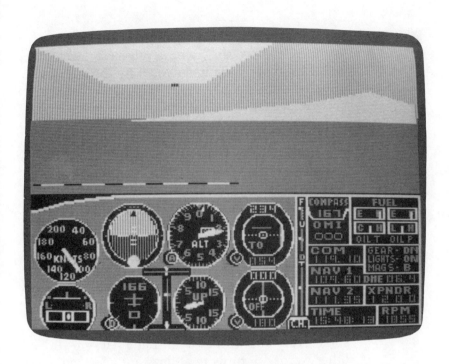

Cutting
Patterns
Spanaway IV

No parameters to set. You set up this mode at the end of the pre-vious adventure. Your flight continues from where you left off.

You've begun your letdown from 4000 feet for a landing at Spanaway. By now you have Tacoma and the airport in sight, so you'll fly the approach visually. Unless you're really skilled at entering a pattern, pause while you consider the following:

You're inbound for runway 16, which is, of course, on a heading of 160 degrees. Looking ahead at the runway—which end will you be landing on?

Well, there's no substitute for being able to figure out by the numbers the traffic pattern around an airport. So it's nice to have a compass rose of some kind, either in the aircraft or in your head.

Unless advised otherwise, or unless other aircraft you see are flying a right-hand pattern, assume every airport flies a left-hand pattern—in other words, all turns to all legs are left-hand turns. And all turns, once you're part of the pattern, are 90-degree turns. Finally, you should enter the pattern on the downwind leg at an angle of 45 degrees.

The downwind leg is the *reciprocal* of the runway heading, the runway heading plus or minus 180 degrees. For Spanaway, downwind is 160 plus 180, or 340 degrees. Or it's 160 minus 180—minus 20 degrees—which is 360 (or 000) minus 20 which is 340. Is that clear?

Next, you have to figure the *entry* heading, which for a left-hand pattern is the downwind heading minus 45 degrees. For a right-hand pattern it's downwind plus 45 degrees. For Spanaway, then, entry is 340 minus 45, or 295 degrees.

Look at your heading indicator. And look at the runway. If you've thought out your landing direction correctly, you know that the downwind leg is this side of the runway. Ideally, you should enter downwind at an early enough point to make your turn and still have time to plan and execute the rest of your landing procedure. You'll want to make some directional changes to get into position. This you do while you're letting down.

The objective is to enter the downwind leg at pattern altitude (we decided on 1400 feet) and pattern airspeed. We'll get to the question of pattern airspeed a little later in this adventure. Right now, you want to get to pattern altitude and into position to enter the downwind leg on a heading of 295 degrees. So unpause now, and go ahead and do that.

Remember, you should change power settings to increase or decrease your rate of descent. As we've learned already, it'll decrease to some extent as your altitude decreases, depending on atmospheric pressure. To increase it, you'll need to decrease your rpm, thus pitching your nose down more steeply.

Though you may turn considerably away from the airport at Spanaway in order to get into your desired entry position, regularly check on where the runway is by using the side views. As you get closer, Spanaway will come into sight on radar, too—an additional help.

If you mess up trying to make this descent and pattern entry, use the reset (called Recall for the IBM) key, and try again. You're not that far out, and reflying it will give you some valuable practice.

In fact, you may want to press the reset now (PrtSc on the IBM, Del on the PCjr, = on the Atari, + on the Commodore 64, and SHIFT-+ on the Apple). Since you've read about getting into the entry position once already, you can start the task earlier, perhaps doing a better job of it.

Watch your altimeter, and adjust your power to vary your descent according to your best judgment as to where and when you're going to enter the pattern.

> **To transition from descent to pattern speed and altitude:**
> 1. **Combine power reductions and trim adjustments to slow both descent rate and airspeed.**
> 2. **Objective is to be straight and level at 80–90 KIAS (Piper), or 60–70 KIAS (Cessna) when you reach pattern altitude.**
> 3. **Coordinate power and nose-up trim to slow aircraft.**
> 4. **Use power for small altitude adjustments.**

This transition takes time, so begin early so that you're straight and level at pattern altitude by the time you enter the downwind leg. Make all elevator adjustments *gradually*. Otherwise, you'll get on a roller coaster. Don't chase the vertical speed indicator. Its middle name is *lag*.

Once you're downwind, get the runway in sight with a direct side view. If you can't see it (except on radar), you're in too close. You may still be able to execute your landing okay, but plan further ahead next time.

As for landing—well, that's for the next adventure. It will help you perfect yours, right here at Spanaway. Even your eyebrows will sprout wings.

Finally
Spanaway V

North Position: 21211
East Position: 6500
Altitude: 1400
Pitch: 359
Bank: 0
Heading: 340
Airspeed: 79 (IBM only)
Airspeed: 84 (all except IBM)
Throttle: 12287 (IBM only)

Throttle: 8191 (all except IBM)
Rudder: 32767
Ailerons: 32767
Flaps: 0
Elevators: 39679 (IBM only)
Elevators: 40959 (all except IBM)
Time: 15:00
Season: 3—Summer
Wind: 4 Kts, 160

Note: It's important to realize that, due to the restrictions of computer simulation, both the Cessna and Piper will fly absolutely straight and level, with any given combination of power and trim, at only one specific altitude.

Immediately, take a 90-degree view off your left wing tip. Then, when the simulator settles down to match the parameters and you're straight and level, pause.

This is the way everything should look when you've entered a pattern and turned downwind perfectly at pattern altitude and pattern airspeed. You're downwind in this case for runway 16 at Spanaway. Because it's a short runway, you can see it all (except the part your wing hides if you're flying the Piper). A longer runway will sometimes require taking 135-degree rear views as well. Note the proximity look, the "fatness," of the runway. Notice, too, its position in relation to your wing.

And look at your panel. Your airspeed indicator reads pattern airspeed (75–85 in the Piper, 60–70 in the Cessna). Your VSI tends to average on the center, or zero, position. Your rpm is your standard slow-flight rpm. You achieved straight and level at that power setting by adjusting elevator trim. You're very stable. And you're ready to execute a precision landing. All the ingredients for developing this precision are in this Spanaway adventure—right here.

Downwind (90-degree view):
Add carb heat opposite end of runway.

Turning base (25-degree turn):
1. Start bank when end of runway is rear of your wing.
2. Take 45-degree view to keep runway in sight.
3. Start roll-out 10 degrees before heading.
4. One notch flaps/one down elevator when wings level. (Press flaps key and elevator-down key simultaneously.)
5. Adjust power and/or trim to suit.

Turning final (keep 45-degree view):
1. Start 25-degree turn as runway leaves view.
2. Adjust bank if needed to keep runway at (diminishing) angle as it crosses your view. (If runway appears straight with 45-degree view, you're beyond it.)
3. Switch to forward view and adjust bank to line up.

Landing:
1. Add full flaps (one down elevator with each notch) to suit approach. This lowers your stalling speed.
2. Adjust power/trim to suit altitude/runway perspective.
3. Watch airspeed and "feel" elevator back in final descent.
4. Touch down just short of, or simultaneously with, stall. (If you get the stall signal, give one notch down elevator.)

No two landings are alike. And landing the simulator while flying an airport pattern is about as tough as they get. By comparison, a straight-in approach from way out is child's play.

The most important turn is, of course, the turn to final, where you want to roll out precisely lined up. It's by far the most difficult—more difficult than if you're flying a real airplane because you lack an instantaneous panoramic view. In the simulator, it's like landing with only one eye (and that one watery).

The preceding guidelines are just that—*guidelines*. There are instructors who will argue with when and where those guidelines suggest you do what. But the important thing is to be consistent. If you always follow the same procedure, your airwork will steadily improve.

Unusual circumstances will dictate departures from procedure. For example, if you have too much altitude downwind, you might want to put on ten degrees of flaps before you turn base, perhaps take off some power, too. Or if you're too low, you can hold off adding carburetor heat until whatever point it suits you, as long as it's *before* you start your power reductions. You can also make more gradual turns to lose altitude gently. The key thing is to avoid abruptness. Do everything with measured precision, anticipating far enough ahead to make it all smooth.

Practice this mode often. Make any adjustments you like to suit your flying style or (good) habits. But once you settle on a procedure that satisfies you, whether it's the one detailed above or your own, follow the procedure all the time. It'll pay off, with the satisfaction that precision brings.

The next and final Spanaway adventure will discuss how to fly a pattern from takeoff to touchdown. And (you're used to this now) by the numbers.

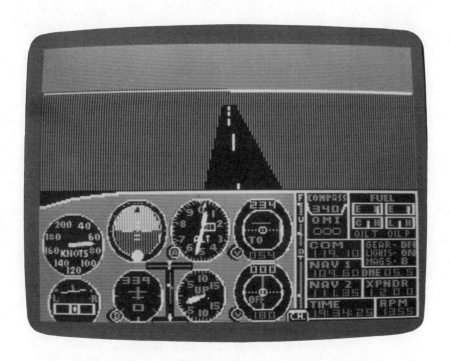

Wrapping the Box

Spanaway VI

North Position: 21218
East Position: 6492
Altitude: 384
Pitch: 0
Bank: 0
Heading: 135
Airspeed: 0
Throttle: 0

Rudder: 32767
Ailerons: 32767
Flaps: 0
Elevators: 32767
Time: 19:00
Season: 3—Summer
Cloud Layer 1: 10000, 8000
Wind: 6 Kts, 156

You had an early dinner so you could get out here and take some pattern practice. It's a nice summer evening. There's an overcast, but it's way up there at 8000 feet. You're at your tie-down position (more about tie-downs in later adventures) near the end of runway 16, but you're not tied down. You're ready to fly.

 You know (from Spanaway I) what your pretakeoff procedures are: ten degrees of flaps. Trim elevator for takeoff (two quick ups). Check carb heat off. And....

An important *and*. It's that we mentally add 400 feet to the airport elevation. The elevation at Spanaway is 385. So we're talking 785. But given some pretty fuzzy television sets and monitors, it's easier to work with closest whole numbers than with exact settings. So think 800 feet.

Airport elevation +400 feet is how high you have to be before making any turns. So that means we'll take off and climb to 800 before we start our turn to the crosswind leg. Then we'll continue climbing to the next important altitude plateau, which is pattern altitude. We know that's airport elevation +1000 feet, which in the case of Spanaway is 1400 feet. So we'll plan to get straight and level when the altimeter reads 1400.

If you're all ready, let's get going.

Use your standard taxi rpm (Cessna 1205, Piper 850) and move ahead, steering as required. Keep rolling as you turn onto the active runway. Add maximum power as you get lined up. Steer if need be as you roll.

Rotate as usual at 60+ in the Cessna, 80 KIAS in the Piper. (If you forgot how to rotate, or what 60+ is, go back to Spanaway I.)

Dump your flaps as soon as your VSI shows 500 fpm up. Then follow this specific procedure to become part of the pattern:

> **Transition to pattern, at pattern speed and altitude:**
> 1. **After flaps up: Reduce rpm to 2105 (Cessna), or 2050 (Piper).**
> 2. **Start trimming to climb 500 fpm.**
> 3. **Turn crosswind at 400 feet AGL.**
> 4. **Take 135-degree view of runway.**
> 5. **Turn downwind when departure end of runway is midscreen.**
> 6. **Switch to 90-degree view of runway.**
> 7. **At pattern altitude** (approximately 1000 AGL), **use power/trim as described earlier to slow-fly straight and level.**

You do all of the above all at once. Well, not exactly all at once. But you have to sort of mix them up and at least *think* about them all together. Sure, this is a busy time, but once you're downwind, you can relax for a few seconds (maybe two, to be exact).

For your reference as you repeatedly (I say repeatedly) practice the transition described by reflying this adventure, here's how you figure headings for the various legs once you know the runway heading (and if you don't know the runway heading by the time you're halfway down it, chop the power, pull over and brake on the grass, put your head in your hands, and just have a good cry. You've earned it).

In a left-hand pattern, subtract 90 from each leg to get the heading for the next leg. Here at Spanaway, for instance, takeoff (or upwind) is heading 160, crosswind is heading 70 (160 − 90), downwind is heading 340 (70 − 90, or −20, thus 360 − 20), base is heading 250 (340 − 90), and final is at heading 160 (250 − 90), the same as takeoff or upwind.

In a right-hand pattern, everything is the same except that you *add* 90 for each leg.

Now, heading downwind at pattern speed and altitude, you realize you've already learned how to do all the rest, from here to touchdown. You've got all the numbers and the procedures down pat. You've put the ribbon on the box.

- Carb heat when you're opposite touchdown point. *Sure.*
- Turn base when runway is rear of wing. *Right.*
- Ten degrees flaps/one down elevator on base leg. *You got 'em.*
- Keep runway in sight with 45-degree view. *Thar she blows!*
- Turn final just before runway end slips from view. *Roger.*
- Simultaneously down elevator/notch of flaps—to full flaps. *All hanging out.*
- Adjust power/elevator to suit as runway comes up. Keep some sky in view else glide too steep. *Gotcha.*
- Watch airspeed with each notch of back pressure. Stall warning horn? Take off a notch of back pressure.
- Just above stall, hang there until you touch. *Lovely.*

So that you can get more pattern practice on each flight, learn how to "touch and go" when you complete a landing. Try this:

> **Transition from touchdown to "touch and go":**
> 1. **Elevator to takeoff trim** (approximate).
> 2. **Flaps up** (zero degrees).
> 3. **Carb heat off.**
> 4. **Advance power to full smoothly.**
> 5. **Normal rotation, and transition to pattern configuration.**

The elevator setting is approximate in the simulator because you're not likely to hit it right on the nose. In an actual aircraft, you'd simply release all the back pressure you'd put on the yoke as you landed. If you remember where your elevator position indicator is when you trim for takeoff (two quick ups, remember?), try to get close to that. It isn't so important, because you'll have takeoff airspeed very soon after you transition from touchdown. But do be *sure* to execute *some* kind of elevator down trim, *and* get the flaps up, *and* get the carb heat off—all smoothly—after you touch and before you go. It's essentially three things, and only three, that you have to remember: (1) elevator, (2) flaps, (3) carb heat. Then it's full power and take off again.

When you learn to fly the "box"—the rectangular pattern around an airport—and fly it well, you'll be flying well indeed. This exercise squeezes all kinds of control challenges into a short period. It's no wonder instructors use it as the basic training procedure for learning to fly. And no wonder that students are soloed soon after they can fly the pattern reasonably well—and long before they really know how to fly from A to B.

Now that you've concluded the Spanaway adventures, you've got a good deal of precision flying technique in your repertoire. Refer to it as needed. Use it to fly everything in this book and to fly the simulator in general. Use the techniques described, or your own version and refinements. It's a far cry from just hacking around. Really. I can see a hint of professionalism in your work already.

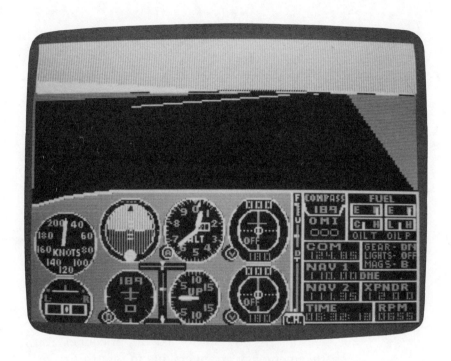

The Arrow

North Position: 15323
East Position: 6085
Altitude: 650
Pitch: 0
Bank: 0
Heading: 190
Airspeed: 0
Throttle: 0
Rudder: 32767

Ailerons: 32767
Flaps: 0
Elevators: 32767 (IBM)
Elevators: 34815 (Apple)
Elevators: 36863 (64 and Atari)
Time: 6:30
Season: 4—Fall
Wind: 8 Kts, 275

Note: Do not *check, set, or otherwise* use *any elevator or any flaps in the course of this flight. They* are disabled *as described.*

You're in a most interesting predicament here at Chino Airport, bright and early on a fine fall morning. You've pulled up to the edge of runway 21, ready to make a normal takeoff. But when you checked your elevator, looking back to be sure it went up and down with your pressure on the yoke, it didn't move. Not a hair up. Not a hair down. You have no elevator control. None.

Furthermore, your flap handle does absolutely nothing. It just loosely swings up and down in your grip. No resistance. No response. As if there's nothing on the other end of it.

Reason tells you not to take off, of course. You made emergency arrangements to rent this crate last night, from an unsavory character who assured you it was airworthy last time he flew it. But he didn't say how long ago that last time was. You paid him in advance—for the round trip. But it looks like you bought a one-way ticket. Still, you absolutely *must* get to San Diego by 7:30 this morning. That's less than an hour from now. And San Diego's about 60 miles away. By the time you taxi back to the hangar, get in your rented car, gas it up, get a road map, and start figuring how to drive to San Diego from way out here, it'll *be* 7:30. And at 7:30, or before, you're supposed to land at Lindbergh Field where your Great-Uncle Larry will be waiting to meet you. Waiting eagerly. He has to catch a 7:45 flight out of San Diego to Outer Mongolia to attend the funeral of your Great-Aunt Atalanta, who was a goodwill worker there, and who has left you a healthy portion of her estate in her will. Great-Uncle Larry has the check for you, and he must put it into your hands in person and give you a kiss from Great-Aunt A. in order to satisfy the stipulations of her will. No Uncle Larry, no kiss, no check. And Uncle Larry, per another stipulation of the will, must spend the remainder of his life in Outer Mongolia carrying on the great work that Great-Aunt Atalanta has begun, or forfeit what the will has in it for him. So this is the first, last, and only chance you have to get that coveted kiss by proxy from Great-Aunt A.

So there's the problem. Or Part One of it. Parts Two and Three are no elevators and no flaps.

Fortunately, *you are not alone* in this airplane. Sitting next to you is a character who watched you awhile, and who then came over to see what the trouble was. He claims he can guide you through the whole flight without elevators or flaps. He also claims he has made a lifetime study of the flight of arrows. And arrows have neither elevators nor flaps. He reminds you rather snootily that in what he calls "this great bird" you have a distinct advantage over an arrow, to wit, adjustable power in flight. The arrow has only its initial power, derived from the stretched bow and bowstring. So it has only one possible trajectory, determined at the instant it's released. You, on the other hand, have variable trajectory. You can go up and come down where you like. And make decisions in flight, all based on variable power.

Either you believe this character, despite his strange appearance and garb (the former haggard and wizardlike, the latter strangely shroudlike and unwashed), or you get no kiss from Great-Uncle Larry. You may imagine it, but there does seem to be a brilliant glitter in the eyes of this arrow man. It's easy to believe he may have genius. What's more, he's going to fly *with* you. It's not like someone giving you a pat on the shoulder and then going for breakfast while you fly off using the cockeyed theory.

Time is short. Life is short. So let's waste no more time.

"Talk me up," you say to the relic beside you. "Talk me up. And then for Pete's sake talk me down!"

And he does. Exactly as follows:

"No worry about elevator. Wind take care of it. Move onto paved place, steer, and give all speed." (You can't rotate, remember. What's to rotate?)

"Now, wait," says The Arrow, when you're aimed down the runway. "Bird fly itself away."

And sure enough, when your airspeed reads something over 100 knots, it does. And you keep full power, waiting for another instruction.

"How high should I climb?" you ask.

"High enough," he mutters. (That, after all, is *your* expertise.)

You decide on 3000 feet. And you tell him.

He asks how you figure out power. And after thinking for a bit you tell him by revolutions per minute in increments of 100.

"Okay," he answers. "When I say less, you give 100 less. When I say more, you give 100 more."

Now that you have this, you feel a little better.

"When you high enough," he says, "give less five times." So at 3000 feet you back off your power five notches.

He looks at you dubiously, as if he doesn't exactly trust you, and says, "If you more high than good, give one less, and if less high than good give one more."

You assume he means get at your desired altitude by a slight change in power setting. So you tell him sure. (He'll learn to trust you, you figure.)

You see the ocean ahead now, and you realize that in all the excitement you've forgotten to get a heading to San Diego. So you tune Mission Bay OMNI on 117.8, center your OBI needle, and bank immediately to get on course.

"You stay straight," says The Arrow, punching his fist vehemently in the direction of the windshield. Apparently the banking makes him uneasy.

You tell him you have to bank the airplane to turn it, but his answering growl is unintelligible.

You notice that Chino is indeed more than 60 miles from San Diego, but if all goes well you should get there in time. At least you'll get over the airport. Getting this turkey on the ground is another matter.

"If too high," repeats The Arrow, "give one less. If too low, give one more." And you keep doing what you have to do powerwise to hold reasonably close to 3000.

Pretty good so far, you think. With nothing but power and aileron, you took off, got to your altitude, got on your heading, and got more or less straight and level.

About when your DME reads 55 miles, your companion mutters that he's hungry.

You tell him sorry. "But when we get to San Diego, sir, I will buy you the biggest breakfast you ever had in your life.

"The sky's the limit," you add. And he looks at you a little funny.

 You tune your COM to San Diego ATIS, 134.8. But you're not in range yet.

You make sure you keep the OBI needle centered, because if you have to do any serious banking, The Arrow might jump out of the airplane. Feeling his center of gravity shift around seems to make him very nervous.

You ask him if he's ever been in an airplane before. But all he answers is "Too high, one less. Too low, one more." It actually sounds comforting, because at least he keeps you honest.

You find yourself wondering how you're supposed to land without elevator. And will it be at 100+ KIAS? You wonder if The Arrow has thought about *that* part of this escapade.

One less. One more. One-way ticket.

Every time he sees a runway, your companion gets very excited. "San Diego, San Diego," he says. But you tell him not yet.

"You *say* San Diego," he says. And you tell him you will.

Meanwhile, you have to keep one more-ing and one less-ing it to hold your altitude. But at least that gives you something to do and keeps your mind off what you're doing.

 About 25 miles out, you try raising the San Diego tower. They give you the runway number, 31. That means downwind on a heading of 130 degrees. It crosses your mind that maybe you should just ditch in the invitingly smooth water down there. But that would mean no inheritance, pure and simple. No way you'll ditch.

You start thinking about your descent for San Diego. Elevation there, you remember, is 15 feet. So you have approximately 3000 feet to lose to touchdown point. (Or smackdown point.) You vaguely remember something you learned way back at Spanaway. About 500 feet per minute and distance to go. So you reach into your flight bag and haul out your trusty *40 More Great Flight Simulator Adventures*. Whereupon your companion starts shouting "No read! No read!" and bangs his fist on the instrument panel.

"Can *you* read?" you ask him in desperation. But he only mutters, "San Diego, San Diego."

"That's San Diego," you tell him, pointing out over the nose.

"How high?" he asks.

And you ask him if he means how high we are now or how high San Diego is? And his answer is "Both."

You tell him, "Three thousand here, no thousand there." You're starting to talk like him.

51

"How long?" he says.

You tell him you have to read the book to find out.

So he says, "How far?" impatiently. Thankfully, your DME has that answer. So you tell him.

"Wait," he says, punching his fist toward the windshield. "Straight arrow, straight arrow," he says. And then adds, "You say 12 miles!"

Now you wonder what he's thinking. Obviously, he wants you to tell him when the DME reads 12 miles out. Can he possibly have a crafty computer in that wizened brain of his? Has he possibly calculated the flight of this arrow right down to the last foot?

Anyway, you have to rely on him. He got you this far.

Meanwhile, you're careful to keep your altitude at 3000, or at least averaging that. And careful to keep that needle on the nose.

 When your DME reads exactly 12, you tell him, "Twelve miles," and then, suddenly, in a kind of stunned way you add, "but that's *nautical* miles!"

His eyes blaze with a fanatic kind of joy. "Two less!" he virtually screams. "Two less!"

Hypnotized, you reduce power by 200 rpm.

Then quite reassuringly, the VSI indicates a descent—at 500 feet per minute. Respectable!

You have the airport in sight, somewhat left of the OMNI bearing, but it isn't very distinct yet.

You decide the best idea is to get on the downwind heading, 130 degrees, and see what develops.

Shortly, you see the runway, and despite shouts of "Straight arrow!" you have to do some banking and turning to get in good position for the downwind leg.

At this point, your companion actually reaches inside his shroudlike garments and pulls forth a miniature arrow, like some kind of token or talisman, and starts stroking it with a kind of fervor.

 You switch in radar and get a look at your relationship to runway 31.

Then you check your altimeter, and, sure enough, there you are, at a very reasonable altitude for a landing. A bit more arrow stroking and you'll be at 1000—pattern altitude. And it's *essential* you get and hold that altitude.

"What now?" you ask The Arrow. But he just says "Wait."

And you judge that maybe you should fly a longer downwind than normal since you'll have to make a power approach so as not to come in too steep.

Your own judgment begins to come seriously into play, as you watch your altimeter and keep check on your relationship to the runway. If you get far enough beyond the touchdown point, then you can make your turns and have a long final to adjust as needed.

You reflect absentmindedly that the DME reads three-odd miles though you're right over the airport. But that, you sagely reason, is because the OMNI station is about three miles away.

"Three miles," you murmur.

"No!" shouts The Arrow, never looking up, but stroking furiously on his totem.

"Okay! Okay!" you shout in return. "I didn't mean three miles away!"

 You decide you'll fly a long enough downwind leg to get the whole runway visible, but pretty small out the rear of this machine. And just when it *is* like that, unaccountably, The Arrow, never looking up, says loudly "One-eighty!"

You do a 180, roll out toward the runway heading, 310, and then work at getting lined up.

All the way in, The Arrow, never looking up from his feverish stroking, keeps saying *one mores* and *one lesses* that you intuitively realize are exactly right for your moment-to-moment situation. Your rate of descent seems mystically to correct itself so that when the wheels touch (right over the centerline, of course) and you chop your power, you have a pretty fast landing, yes, but you're amazingly safe and sound—you're there! You made it!

You extend your hand to shake the hand of The Arrow, and a shudder goes through you.

He is *not there*. Nowhere to be seen.

All that's left is the token, the talisman, lying there on the right seat. The Arrow.

You get the coveted, mutually embarrassing buss on the check from Great-Uncle Larry. But all that's postlude. Without The Arrow, the morning has lost its grand excitement. You deeply regret not having the opportunity, once Uncle Larry's flight has departed for Outer Mongolia, to buy breakfast for that shriveled, blazing-eyed old wizard. It would have been easy to keep your promise to buy him all he could eat. With the $40.27 Great-Aunt Atalanta left you in her will.

Bull's-Eye

North Position: 17560
East Position: 22134
Altitude: 4500
Pitch: 0
Bank: 0
Heading: 200
Airspeed: 122 (IBM only)
Airspeed: 126 (all except IBM
Throttle: 23551
Rudder: 32767

Ailerons: 32767
Flaps: 0
Elevators: 32767 (IBM)
Elevators: 34815 (Apple)
Elevators: 36863 (64 and Atari)
Time: 10:20
Season: 4—Fall
Cloud Layer 1: 3000, 400
Shear Zone Altitude 1: 5000
Wind: 3 Kts, 230

The weather being what it is, your decision is to get on the ground as soon as possible.

 You contact the Martha's Vineyard tower on 121.4.

The ceiling they quote you is pretty unbelievable—worse than the weather report. But, fortunately, the Martha's Vineyard ILS is in operation, so that's obviously the way to go.

The tower gave you the ILS frequency, 108.7, so you crank it into NAV 1 and then tune NAV 2 to the Martha's Vineyard VOR, 108.2. You find you're well to the left of the 240-degree radial, and you want to get on it as soon as possible since you're only 15 or so miles out and you'll be landing on runway 24. You set the OBI on NAV 2 to 240, and turn right to a heading of 330. That's like putting yourself on base for runway 24.

Sure enough, the needle on your number-two OBI comes into action in just a few minutes, followed shortly by the ILS centerline needle. When that's centered, you turn to track it and get down to the business of your approach.

 You want to get into slow flight and set up a descent rate of about 500 feet per minute, these being the ideals for an ILS approach. So you use a combination of power reduction and up elevator trim until you get the desired readings. They aren't achieved all at once. As you reduce power, you'll start descending. But to hold the rate of descent at 500 fpm, you'll find you need to keep trimming. At the same time, you want to decrease your speed. So you keep trading off one against the other, the objective being to get the aircraft in balance at a steady rate of descent and the KIAS you've established for slow flight.

Then your job is to keep both ILS needles crosshaired on the center of the instrument. Adjust power as needed all the way down to stay on the glide slope. At 3000 feet, you'll be in the overcast. Don't let the centerline indicator get away. Make minor heading adjustments immediately if you stray from it by even a degree. Your primary instruments now are the OBI and the artificial horizon, and your primary control is the throttle. If the OBI display looks right, your wings are level (or in a gentle bank if you're trying to center the needle), and your nose is just a bit below the horizon. You're right on. Stay there.

Try to anticipate the glide slope and centerline needles. The centerline in particular will get more critical as you get closer to the runway.

Shortly after the marker tones wake you from your hypnosis, you'll break out of the overcast and see the bull's-eye you set up on your OBI come to life in three dimensions. Doesn't that green look awfully welcome?

Time Warps

North Position: 17419
East Position: 7402
Altitude: 410
Pitch: 0
Bank: 0
Heading: 150
Airspeed: 0
Throttle: 0

Rudder: 32767
Ailerons: 32767
Flaps: 0
Elevators: 32767
Time: 6:28
Season: 2—Spring
Wind: 5 Kts, 150

Be sure your heading is 149–150, because there's a runway out there and you're on it. Take my word. Nature just hasn't turned on the lights yet. Just wait for a minute or two until 6:30.

Meanwhile—courtesy of the Dawn Patrol—if you're flying a Cessna, your airplane has just got a brand-new paint job.

 At daylight, take a 45-degree look to your left. And while you're looking around, just continue to rotate counterclockwise through all your views. Anything look familiar?

That mark on the mountain. Now is that for real? Are we really *there*?

If we are, how come we're in an unmodified airplane? (That is, except for the paint job on the Cessna.)

If we're way back then, how come we have a full complement of instruments? And if this is the Europe of 1917, how come we have OMNI? And if it's 1917, how come *W* doesn't start a war? (Try pressing that key.)

Take a look on radar. There's the river. Sure looks like the WWI scenario. But if it is, we snuck into it before dawn, and with a fully modern airplane. Neat trick.

But maybe this just *looks* like the 1917 thing. If there's no war, then maybe we've come back nearly three-quarters of a century later? Why? To reminisce?

Wonder if we can fly away from this European base. Maybe to somewhere else in Europe. After all, things should be more developed now.

Let's give it a whirl. Let's take off and fly this heading and see where it takes us.

Go.

Our cruise altitude will be 3000 feet.

 As you climb, take a look directly behind you. Doesn't look like a war zone. Maybe pressing the R key will give us a war report. It's supposed to. Does your screen say *Sorry, there will be no war today.* Or, *Sorry, you're about 70 years too late. Where you been?*

Hit X and maybe we can drop a bomb on the wiseacre. But X doesn't work either. So, just fly.

Looks pretty monotonous ahead. Just ground and sky. Not one skyscraper. Not even a condominium.

But we don't give up easily, do we?

 Look behind you once in a while, just to see whether an enemy fighter is sneaking up on you. Also to watch the past disappear.

We have a DME, but nothing to tune to to see how far away we are. From nowhere or anywhere. Maybe this is what they called no man's land.

Hang on to that 3000-feet altitude, and a heading around 150. Don't touch the ailerons at all.

 Somewhere around 7:00 a.m. (more like 6:45 if you're flying with an Apple version), you'll notice (behind you) that the war zone, if that's what it was, evaporates. It doesn't just shrink like most scenics. It just puffs away.

So now, there's nothing at all, right?

Well, not quite.

Take a look out your left side. And then out your right.

What's *that*? Another WWI zone?

Looks suspiciously like the one we left way back there, doesn't it? So how did *that* spring up? It even has a river. And the same mountains. But we've been flying away from it for nearly a half hour. During which it looks like we flew right back to it.

Now, if it's a mirror image of where we were, how come it's off to our right instead of straight ahead of us?

Or maybe there are four mirror images.

Look out the left side.

Nope.

Maybe there are three. Let's keep flying straight ahead. This could get interesting.

 Keep looking around at regular intervals. We don't want to miss anything. That second battle zone will begin to get smaller. And what then?

It didn't take all that long to get to Europe 1917, number 2. Just about as soon as number 1 evaporated.

Well, now number 2 evaporated! Keep a sharp lookout. All sides.

What do you know about that! Maybe four mirror images it is. And maybe we *will* come back to where we started. And Einstein was right after all.

Fly, my friend. Fly this weird world. Fly this weird warp or woof or whatever. We may uncover the secret of the universe out here. Or some great truth.

Be sure this time, as Europe 1917, number 3, or Europe 2017, number 9, begins to shrink, that you keep your eye on it via a rear view and actually see it evaporate.

Meanwhile, consider that we've seen this piece of scenic wonderland three times so far, and from three different perspectives. We seem to be in a land of mirrors. Perhaps of infinite mirrors.

Do you suppose these places are test scenics Bruce Artwick put out here, far from everything, figuring no one would ever discover them? Places where he could practice his wizardry? Where he could try things out? And if so, what things?

Keep watching that number 3. This may be the last of the mirror images, and when it goes we may—just may—be able to land straight ahead on the runway we left at dawn.

When number 3 is blown away, hold your breath a second. Then look all around again. Until you see it.

Guess we're on a long final, hmmm?

We'll have to clear the mountain top, of course. But then, what would you like to bet we'll be exactly lined up for runway 15, Europe 1917?

Keep on flying at 3000. Straight ahead. Looks like we might just clear through that little notch.

If you're not at 3000, use this time to get there. And stay there. And if you messed around with aileron and aren't heading 150, maybe you'll just have to start all over again.

Do you think we'll clear the mountaintop? Is the peak straight ahead now instead of the notch? Or are we aimed a little below the peak, on the slope?

Later...

Begins to look kind of high up, that mountain, doesn't it? But we're committed. Whatever happens, happens.

Now it doesn't look too good. Maybe you want to pause the flight here for a few moments and weigh it all.

But can that mountain be above 3000 feet? That little mountain, in that neat little stage setting? All done with mirrors?

Fly on, at 3000 feet.

Soon, the blue sky is disappearing from view. All of that blue is gone. Only the wall, that wall we know is paper thin.

No chance now. The mountain is no illusion.

But after it happens, we're again—mercifully—on the runway. Runway 15. The same. And it's dawn again. Like waking from a bad dream. Glad to see the runway and the dawn.

We thought, as we flew along there earlier, that we might uncover some great secret or some big truth in this mysterious time warp of mirrors within mirrors. Europe 1917, number 1, 2, 3, 4. Or is it really 4, 3, 2, 1?

Yes. So there *is* a secret, and a big truth, if you think about it. All those war zones, as we flew, just evaporated. And that's the way it should be. That's what this phenomenon in the simulator is telling us. Either we evaporate—from our eyes and minds and the whole scene—every Europe 1917 or Europe 2017 or whatever, or we'll be evaporated ourselves.

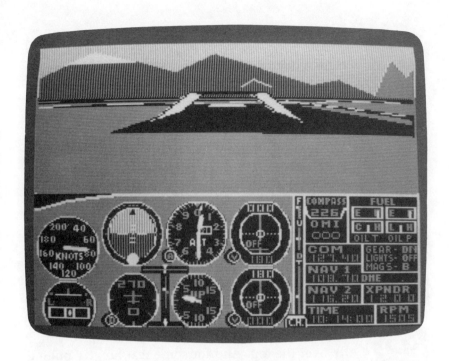

Hangin' Out

North Position: 17417
East Position: 7452
Altitude: 475
Pitch: 359
Bank: 0
Heading: 270
Airspeed: 84 (IBM only)
Airspeed: 92 (all except IBM)
Throttle: 12287 (IBM only)
Throttle: 11307 (all except IBM)

Rudder: 32767
Ailerons: 32767
Flaps: 0
Elevators: 37631 (IBM)
Elevators: 36607 (Apple)
Elevators: 40703 (64 and Atari)
Time: 10:13
Season: 3—Summer
Wind: 2 Kts, 265

Don't touch the controls. Sit this one out for a couple of passes. After all, you just came back from a dogfight with Baron Manfred von Richthofen, and the good news is you survived. You even have an idea you put a bullet through his fuselage, while he was on his back at the top of an Immelmann. No wonder you feel a bit cocky.

They're glad to see you back here at home base, and the squadron leader will forgive your high-spirited antics.

Fly this a few times, and take a look out the side and out the rear. The 45- and 90-degree views are particularly dramatic. You're close to the floor, but there's very little clearance between you and the roof.

After a few passes, take over and pull up so you fly over the top. And for some real fun, try pulling up just enough and then cutting your power to skim the roof with your wheels. But, careful, or you'll sink right in. And the squadron has no airplanes to spare.

Waterline

North Position: 21412
East Position: 6476
Altitude: 482
Pitch: 0
Bank: 0
Heading: 167
Airspeed: 0
Throttle: 0

Rudder: 32767
Ailerons: 32767
Flaps: 0
Elevators: 32767
Time: 15:00
Season: 4—Fall
Cloud Layer 1: 10000,7500
Wind: 0 Kts, 0

While you're waiting for takeoff here at Bremerton National, switch in your radar and adjust it until you see four chunks of water and, to your left, most of the metropolitan area of Seattle.

Ahead of you is Henderson Bay, and the little pencil line at two o'clock leads to Hood Canal, with Dabob Bay at about five o'clock. Much of the Puget Sound area, between where you are and where Seattle is, is reduced to thin pencil lines in this graphic. But just to your left is an unseen little sluiceway where there's a navy shipyard and museum, and the WWII battleship U.S.S. *Missouri* is on display. The Japanese formally surrendered on "Mighty Mo" in 1945, ending the Second World War.

You have no weather report, and there's no tower. What you *do* know is that there was a breeze hitting your face before you climbed in the airplane, and that it was coming from the south. So we'll take off on runway 19. Then we'll follow the little water line over on the right to Hood Canal. We'll track the canal north to Dabob Bay.

 Go through your pretakeoff procedure, taxi into position, and hold for a moment while you read the following.

We'll climb straight out and plan to level off and get into slow flight at an altitude of 1500 feet. As you climb, then, pay attention to your altitude. Take a right front view and look for the little pencil line that leads to Hood Canal. You'll be able to see it while runway 19 is still beneath you. Turn and line up with this strip of water and slowly fly along it at your altitude of 1500. Use radar, if you like, to help you do this.

Go ahead and roll.

Once you have the thin waterway on a straight line ahead of you, you'll see that it bears about 225 degrees. Hood Canal is the good-sized body of water at the end of this line. Just about where the pencil line starts is the town of Belfair and a state park of the same name. Five miles or so farther along is Twanoh State Park on your left.

Once you have the canal clearly visible, fly a bit to the left and pick it up where it starts. Use your right side views to see the perspective of the water and judge your turn. Use radar if it helps. Note how the little pencil line of water connects into the big picture. On the north shore, just about at that point, is the town of Tahuya, and on the south shore is Union. Below your aircraft as you turn to track the canal are Snohomish Indian Reservation and Potlatch State Park.

After you're settled on the canal heading (about 12 degrees), take a view off to your right. That's Mount Rainier, a good 60 miles away. Look directly behind you, too. Pretty piece of water, isn't it? Two other little towns you'll pass are, in order, Hoodsport and Lilliwaup. Don't you love some of these names?

The canal is so straight you might want to vary your flight a bit, lining up with and flying along the east and/or west banks for a while. You can't see U.S. 101 in the simulation, but it parallels the west bank.

The highways visible way over there around Seattle are Interstate 5 and Interstate 405.

When you're about three-quarters of the way to Dabob Bay, you'll be able to spot Bremerton National off your right wing tip.

But what happened to Mount Rainier? It's a cloudy day, sure, but it isn't that cloudy, is it? They give you a runway and take away your mountain.

As you near the bay, the geography off to your left is Dosewallips State Park, part of the Olympic National Forest. The forest stretches all the way from here almost to the northern border of the state. There are spruce trees and Douglas firs in there high as 25-story buildings.

 Getting close to Dabob Bay, you'll see another pencil line of water splitting off from it, just to the right of where the land juts forward. That's more of Hood Canal, and we'll fly over there and follow it.

As you make your turn, you'll be passing Scenic Beat State Park on your right and the little town of Seabeck.

 Keep an eye out to your right, and you may see a mountain magically materialize on the landscape. Around the same time, someone will dump a whole lot of landfill into Dabob Bay.

But follow the canal line anyway. It's not the one that veers off to the left, but the one ahead, bearing about 5 to 10 degrees. The large body of water up ahead is Admiralty Inlet, part of Puget Sound. And on its southern bank, to the right of the canal, is another Indian reservation, Port Gamble. Those mountains off to your right are part of the Cascade Range, far to the east.

The canal will shift around a bit, but just keep the point where it joins Admiralty Inlet ahead of you. As you get beyond that point, go into radar mode and you'll pick up an airport to your right. That's Snohomish County.

Paine VOR is right there, so tune your NAV to it—114.2. Center the OBI needle and take up the heading you read out.

Contact Snohomish ATIS, 128.65, to check weather and which way they're landing. (They tell you zero wind, but you remember that breeze from the south at Bremerton.) Elevation is 603 MSL, so your altitude, if you're still at 1500, is fine for the pattern. And your airspeed, if you're still in slow flight, is fine for pattern airspeed, too.

They tell you they're landing on runway 3 (the actual runway heading is closer to 20 degrees than 30 degrees), and there's no traffic, so why not ask permission to enter the left-hand pattern on base leg? That means just an easy right turn to about 100 degrees, followed by a left turn to final when you're ready. If the tower doesn't answer no matter how loud you shout, go ahead and do it anyway. They deserve that for making you land downwind.

Skoal!

North Position: 21616
East Position: 6737
Altitude: 137
Pitch: 0
Bank: 0
Heading: 340
Airspeed: 0
Throttle: 0

Add for this mode:
Wind Level 1: 25 Kts, 180
Shear Zone Altitude 1: 3000

Rudder: 32767
Ailerons: 32767
Flaps: 0
Elevators: 32767
Time: 5:00
Season: 3—Summer
Wind: 5 Kts, 340

This is Arlington Municipal Airport, Arlington, Washington, a town of 33,000-odd souls some 30-odd miles from the border of British Columbia. Most important, it's the northernmost airport in the simulator world.

Which is lucky, because we want to be as close to where we're going as possible. And we're going north. Indeed, before we take off, I suggest you get yourself a pair of gloves, some earmuffs, and heavy clothing. Not to mention a gallon vacuum jug of hot coffee. Because we're going to take off and fly to—or at least toward—believe it or not, the North Pole.

"Baloney!" you say.

That's no way to talk. Have I ever let you down before? Is there anything that says we can't do it?

Look at it this way. Well, no, we'll look at it that way later. We'll have plenty of time for chit-chat since we have a long way to go.

 Let's go ahead and get started while it's nice and early. Notice we have a nice, gentle headwind for takeoff—right down the runway. Then above 3000 feet, we pick up a 25-knots-per-hour tail-wind, which will make our flight *much* shorter.

Trust me. Roll 'em.

Take off, turn to a due north heading as you pass through 500 feet, and level off at 4000. From that altitude we should be able to see pretty well in all directions. And can't you imagine how scenic this flight will be?

I'll pick up the conversation as soon as you have 4000 feet and your heading.

Look at it this way. (Don't bother to pause, because this flight may be a long one. You can read this, and perhaps the last three weeks of the *Wall Street Journal*, while you fly.) As I said, look at it this way—you're at 4000 feet, on a heading of 000, in a 100 percent reliable airplane. You have a head start on the daylight and a lot of time to think. You're heading into the Great Unknown. Like Admiral Byrd, Lindbergh, or Amelia Earhart. You're doing this in a Great Cause, a Heroic Cause. You're flying into the Great Unknown for the same reason that Hillary climbed that mountain—because it's there.

Now that should be reason enough for any red-blooded American. You could be about to make history. Or, at the least, you're meeting a great challenge, doing a great deed of derring-do.

But wait, there's more.

 First, though, let's make our last contact with simulator civilization. You're somewhere east of the northernmost VOR station on your charts— Bay View. Set your NAV to 108.2 and see how far away it is. It'll keep getting farther away. But at least it'll give us something that's alive on the radio for a while.

We *know* there's no North Pole in the simulator world. We're not kidding ourselves. We're not going to see a lot of ice and snow or any little flags down there even if we fly all day and all night.

But one thing is virtually certain. We'll see *something*. And unless we take this flight, we'll never know *what*, will we? So all your friends who've never flown more than ten miles from Meigs will wind up envying you. All those arm-

chair pilots without the *Right Stuff*. If we can fly to
the moon in a spacecraft, we can certainly fly to
the North Pole in this simulator.

And something else. It stands to reason that the
simulator world doesn't actually end. If it did,
what would happen? Would the computer shut itself off? Would we get a disclaimer of some kind
on the screen? Something like, *Sorry, but you can't
get there from here.* Would the plane stop dead in
its tracks and fall out of the sky? This isn't a
movie, it's a simulation of real geography. There
can't be a specific end, any more than space can
suddenly stop. What *is* the simulator world? A big
sphere? If that's so, then we're on the outside of
it, or the inside of it. Either case, it curves back on
itself, and we'll get to the southernmost extremities by flying to the northernmost. It shouldn't
even take too long. If it's flat, like a big sheet of
paper, then the same thing will result, except we'll
fly off the top and fly in again on the bottom. If
it's a Möbius strip, same thing. Or what if it's a
piece of paper printed on both sides, with, say,
Seattle on one side and New York/Boston on the
other? Maybe we'll fly from Arlington Municipal
to JFK in an hour or so. Faster than a speeding
bullet.

Very green out there, isn't it, if you have daylight by now. And we've put some distance between us and Bay View. My DME reads 77.1 right
now (just so we'll have at least one last thing to
compare as we fly).

But don't be a quitter. This could be the most
important flight you'll ever make.

Check your altitude once in a while. Stay at
4000 and keep your heading. Look around once in

a while. The populated area we've left is still visible out the back at 83 miles from Bay View. I have a hunch something—I don't know what—may happen when that little strip of something disappears.

I know you're looking at nothing but green, and it gets pretty boring. But the Lone Eagle looked at nothing but blue for many long hours. And he couldn't even see out the front.

DME's still reading out, at—oops, it isn't any more. Think it was 89 something. So now we're at a plateau of some kind. I can't tell you where I am. But we still have a reference—old Father Time.

My time right now is 5:50. I still have that strip of world behind me and nothing ahead of me.

Want to send out for a sandwich? We certainly can't take our eyes off the screen, with all the excitement going on there.

Time—5:52. And the strip is still visible out the rear. We've not slipped the bonds of Artwick yet!

At 5:53:22, I'm looking out the rear, and, peculiar though it is, the thin strip of civilization is at the top of the horizon. It has nowhere to go now but up, into the sky, in other words, out of the simulation. When you get near that time, keep looking out back and see what happens.

But now, as I'm getting back up to 4000, the altitude gives me a higher perspective, and the strip is a hair below the horizon. So whatever's going to happen isn't going to happen just yet.

Now I'm level at 4000, the time is 5:58, and the strip is about its own width under the rear horizon. It's about a half inch off the left of my fin, just sitting there.

Now it's exactly even with the horizon, at 5:58:31. Something's *bound* to happen now. Except it doesn't seem to know exactly where it is, because it slips back into the world by a hair again. Anyway, its time is definitely short. Watch with me.

And when it pops off, be ready to take an immediate look out front and see if anything pops on.

At 6:14, by my clock, the strip popped into oblivion. And I take a quick look out front. And I see something.

Lots of green. Left and right front views, too. Green. I remember that "Sesame Street" song, "It Isn't Easy Being Green." It isn't easy looking at it either.

But fly on. We've only been out an hour by my clock. Your clock, of course, may be slightly different, depending on how you took off and got to your heading.

I'll keep looking out both sides now at regular intervals. Wondering when I'll get to the edge of the piece of paper.

Of course, there's a possibility that we could actually be flying on the other side, or into the opposite edge, of the piece of paper, or crossing a seam in the sphere, and still see nothing because we're there, but we're not near anywhere. If you follow my meaning.

I think I'll get out my Los Angeles chart and see if I can raise any OMNI stations down there. Let's see. Southernmost is Mission Bay, 117.8. Tune to that. Nothing? Let's try Santa Catalina, 111.4.

Well, we're not 80–85 miles from either of them. What else have we? Nothing in the Los Angeles area.

So let's move east and try the Chicago area. Get out another chart. Champaign VORTAC, 110.0.

Nothing.

One more possibility. New York/Boston. VORTAC Kennedy, 115.9. No such luck.

Try Martha's Vineyard, though I have no idea why, 108.2.

Well, maybe we can try tuning OMNIs at the *top* of those areas. Nothing says we have to come in at their southern extremities.

I'll try one, anyway. Back to—well, it wouldn't be Seattle, would it? So try top of Los Angeles? That doesn't make any sense.

Anyway, Fillmore, 112.5.

Kind of dead out here, isn't it?

Once in a while, anyway, I'm going to try to raise Mission Bay.

Really a world apart out here. Why bother to put all this nothing geography in this thing? You could put ten thousand Ringling Bros. and Barnum & Bailey Circuses out there. And still have room for Asia.

My time is your time. I mean mine is 6:21. These songs keep going through my head.

Nothing out front. Nothing out left side. Nothing out right side. Nothing down.

I hope you're not beginning to think I've led you on a wild-goose chase. You enjoy flying, don't you? If not, why did you invest all that money for a computer to fly this simulator?

So you're flying. So enjoy.

Time is 6:26. We haven't even been out an hour and a half.

I'm beginning to wonder whether that due north heading made any sense. My geography isn't all that great. And maybe, even if this simulator world is all on a piece of paper, our great circle route has got us into Idaho or some place like that.

And we could keep flying in great circles all around the globe for three or four days, just missing exciting places by a few hundred miles.

I wonder what North Position and East Position readings are right now. With a little clever research, that could give us a clue as to where we are in a general way. But that would be cheating. Admiral Byrd didn't have an editor he could check with. Or Lindbergh either.

It's 6:32:14, and I'm still tuned to Mission Bay. Come to think of it, that's Lindbergh's own namesake, San Diego International—Lindbergh Field.

But a lot of help that is now.

Nothing out front, nothing out right, nothing out left, nothing out anywhere.

I wish you'd make some conversation. I mean, you just sit there. Like this was all *my* fault. I didn't design the simulator. Or the world, either.

Go ahead and quit if you want to. Go ahead, go back to your cozy Meigs field and practice crashing. See if I care.

If Eli Whitney had quit, we wouldn't have the cotton gin.

I would never have suggested we try to fly, say, from New York to Los Angeles, over the regular airline routes anyway. But this idea of flying off one edge and onto another seemed reasonable to me. Or flying around and upside down from one place inside a globe to another place on the other side of the globe.

One thing is sure—if you throw in the towel, you'll never be able to discover what the rest of us are going to discover on this flight. Because I don't intend to reveal the coordinates of our destination when we discover it.

If you're really dying to see something—anything—take a look straight down.

If you're flying a Cessna, that's your wheel. And if you're flying a Piper, you tell me what it is.

And while you're looking at it, I'll tip you off to a real fun thing if you're flying Cessna. Retract your wheels. Just for a second. And then put them down again. Wasn't that fun? That alone could make this whole trip worthwhile.

(If you're in Piper, I don't know what to tell you to do.)

It's 6:51:01 (or just was) by my clock. I'm going to try tuning Bloomington VOR, 108.2. Don't ask me why. And don't bother doing it.

I chose flying north because I figured that would be a shorter distance around than flying east or west. And I chose not to slew for a number of reasons, not the least of which is that I subscribe to the realism of the simulator.

It's coming up on 7:00 a.m. At that time, we'll have been flying two hours. I'm tuning the NAV back to Mission Bay, 117.8 (if one could be said to be "tuning" anything out here). But I think we're way east of San Diego. Not to mention north of it.

I wonder how long it would take to try to raise every OMNI station there is. There must be some kind of solution to this thing.

It's about 7:07. And by my best estimate we're now over the Galapagos Islands.

The Galapagos Islands are an island group with an area of 2966 square miles. Situated in the Pacific Ocean, 650 miles west of the mainland, the islands have a population of 2400. That's more than one square mile per person—man, woman, and child.

Starting with 108.0 and advancing slowly by 0.05's, I can tune through the entire NAV frequency spectrum. Slowly, and see if anything at all comes alive.

No, I *didn't* suggest you do this. I have no control over your behavior. But I assure you, if I *do* find something, I *won't* spoon-feed the numbers to you.

Anyway, do you have a better idea?

Well, it doesn't take as long as you might think to exhaust the OMNI possibilities.

And since you haven't made any wisecracks for quite a while, I do feel obligated to tell you something. That something is—we're not within 85 or 90 miles of anywhere at all, if you want to believe the OMNI. We're nowhere—we won't see a landmark, let alone recognize it, for a long, long time.

It's now 7:36:31, and as far as I'm concerned, we made it.

I'm perfectly aware that you might not recognize that fact, but just bear with me, and follow my instructions exactly.

 Reduce your power to set up a descent rate of 500 feet per minute. Don't mess around with your elevator. Leave it where it was when you were straight and level (for the last two and a half hours). And don't make any additional rpm adjustments. At lower altitudes, your rate of descent will slowly diminish by itself.

Just let the plane descend of its own accord.

We're going to make an airline approach and landing, nice and flat. We want the airspeed we have, because it's very icy down there. Higher airspeed will give us better control on the ice. We don't want to be sliding all over the place, do we?

If you should get to where you're descending at lower than 50 feet per minute, of course, take off a notch of rpm. We don't want to come in *that* flat. But if you're descending at all, keep it that way. The plane will land itself.

And the landing alone will make aviation history. We will get a special certificate from the Federal Aviation Administration, commemorating the longest final approach ever flown in a single-engine aircraft. Not to mention we'll be in the *Guinness Book of Records.*

When your VSI goes to zero, you'll know you're on the ground. Cut your power, but don't use brakes. Let the airplane slide to a stop on its own.

Never made a smoother landing, did you? No bounce. No wild oscillations.

Look around you. If you're flying a Cessna, there may be a funny something about your wings.

Without your being aware of it, I've carefully tricked you into flying to the one place you never believed we'd actually reach. Where I jokingly said, way back at the beginning, that we obviously couldn't actually get to.

But we made it. Plus or minus no more than 187 feet in any direction (depending upon minor differences in our on-board clocks as compared to Greenwich mean and other times, and on how closely your flight duplicated the one described), you're sitting on, and looking at, none other than the *North Pole!*

I appreciate that you're probably feeling cold up here, and the cold is creeping into the cockpit.

But against that cold, may I offer you my sincerest, most heartfelt, and very, very warmest—congratulations!

Island
Getaway
Tie-Down I

North Position: 17352
East Position: 21750
Altitude: 105
Pitch: 0
Bank: 0
Heading: 280
Airspeed: 0
Throttle: 0

Rudder: 32767
Ailerons: 32767
Flaps: 0
Elevators: 32767
Time: 6:30
Season: 2—Spring
Wind: 0 Kts, 0

This and the following two adventures introduce the concept of *tie-downs*. A tie-down is a position at an airport where your aircraft is normally parked and lashed to stakes or something in the ground, with wheels chocked and—you hope—no For Sale sign stuck on the fuselage.

The idea is that you can have your Cessna or Piper parked at your own personal tie-down at any and all airports of your choice in the simulator world. Then, anytime you want to take a flight from a given location, you load the mode (which you've saved on disk) and there's your plane, parked in your own personal spot, ready for you to climb in and go.

The other side of the coin is that, when you fly to or back to an airport where you have a tie-down, you land and then taxi to that spot before you shut down. It's all part of the realism. Whoever heard of landing at an airport and leaving the plane on the runway?

Some of the desirable attributes of a simulator tie-down include:

• Centrality to runways we'll use, without necessarily favoring any given strip.
• Realistic view out front when we enter the mode.
• Optimum radar view for orienting ourselves to runways, taxiways, fuel stations, and so on.
• Good nighttime aspect, with good taxiway visibility.

Our present tie-down is at Block Island State Airport, Block Island, Rhode Island.

Since a tie-down airport is a form of "home" airport, we also want to have the vital statistics about it jotted down somewhere. Such as:

> **Runways:** 10/28 (2500 × 100)
> **Elevation:** 105
> **Tower:** 123.0
> **VOR:** None (meaning no OMNI station within a ten-mile radius, such as you could home on when inbound)

This type of information is useful to have in a black book in your flight bag to refer to whenever you're flying. From it, you can pick a tie-down airport of convenience when you feel like landing, and you'll have vital statistics for contacting the tower, getting to pattern altitude, and making your approach.

You'll also want to know something about the area surrounding each "home" airport, so you'll feel more at home. Like:

Block Island is in Block Island Sound (Atlantic Ocean) approximately 14 miles off the southern coast of Rhode Island. It is about 16 miles east and a bit north of Montauk Point, the easternmost tip of Long Island. Nearest airports are Martha's Vineyard VOR (108.2), and Chester, 12 miles northeast of Madison VOR (110.4). Farthest airports are La Guardia or Kennedy via Hampton (113.6), Deer Park (111.2), and La Guardia (113.1); or via Kennedy (115.9).

Most scenic flights: west over Long Island or its north or south shore; east over the water to Martha's Vineyard, paralleling Rhode Island shoreline.

Select one of these flights, think up a surface wind and some weather conditions for the editor, and go flying when you finish this adventure.

Location and taxiing information. You're parked on the grass and parallel to runway 28, visible on the left of your windshield. The tarmac ahead of you leads to the fuel area, also visible ahead.

For runway 28, do a 180 to the left, taxi to the end of the runway, and do another 180 over the numbers.

For runway 10, taxi straight ahead on the grass, crossing both taxiways, and do a 180 to your left over the numbers. Traffic permitting, you may also taxi on the runway itself, or in the case of runway 10, follow the taxiway (between the blue lights at dusk or night) through the fuel area, then left, then right along the strip to the numbers.

This is a short runway, so don't waste any.

Once you have a tie-down like this on a custom disk, you can load it and change the time, the wind direction, the weather—any or all three of them to suit yourself.

And remember, whenever you land here, go back to *your* tie-down. If you find some other aircraft parked there, you can let the air out of its tires. Or at least leave a nasty note.

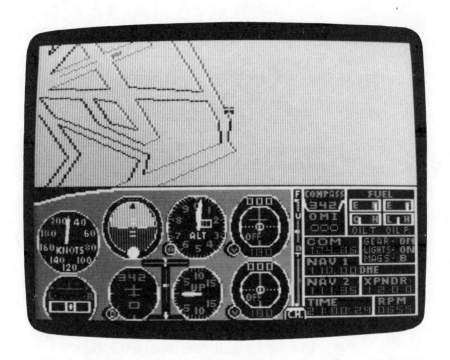

Corner on JFK
Tie-Down II

North Position: 17031
East Position: 21073
Altitude: 12
Pitch: 0
Bank: 0
Heading: 320
Airspeed: 0
Throttle: 0

Rudder: 32767
Ailerons: 32767
Flaps: 0
Elevators: 32767
Time: 21:00
Season: 3—Summer
Wind: 0 Kts, 0

John F. Kennedy International (JFK), New
York, New York
Runways: 4R/22L (8400 × 150)—Unpaved,
no centerline

14/32 (2560 × 75)—Unpaved, no
centerline

Elevation: 12
Tower: 119.1
VORTAC: Kennedy—115.9

 Switch radar on and zoom around a bit. At the
higher altitudes, consider how tiny you are way
over there at the edge of everything.

JFK is a mammoth airport with ten runways, but
light aircraft are assigned one of the four shown
above. The airport area is bordered on the south
and west by Jamaica Bay, though the detail
doesn't show up in the simulator. To the east is
the Borough of Brooklyn and to the north the Borough of Queens. Long Island stretches off to the
west. The nearest airports are LaGuardia to the
north (VOR 113.1) and Republic, a few miles west
of Deer Park VOR (111.2). The farthest airports
are Logan International in Boston and Martha's
Vineyard off the southern Massachusetts coast.
(Consult your chart for the numerous OMNI fixes
along these routes.)

Most scenic flight. Northeastward to see the
Statue of Liberty and Manhattan (World Trade
Center, Empire State Building, Manhattan Bridge,
Central Park), beautiful anytime of day or night.
Make one of these flights when you finish this
adventure. Or take off, fly the pattern (touch and
go if you like), then land and try to taxi back to
your tie-down.

Location and taxiing information. You are parked for any of the runways you'll be using, at the extreme northeast corner of the airport complex. Radar shows you're just to the right of the end of runway 32, and that's the runway you see to the left out your windshield. Also on radar, in a fairly close-in view (or seen with a left rear view out your cabin windows), the wavy lines at seven o'clock (blue lights at dusk and night) mark a short taxiway which connects runways 32 and 22. For their reciprocals, 14 and 4, just taxi alongside either, and then do a 180 to get lined up.

The choice of dusk for this tie-down mode sets you up for flying over Manhattan, first at dusk, and then if you're in the air long enough, at night. Of course, you can change the time or season as you like.

To add interest to a tie-down mode, go into the editor and set any random wind and wind direction that comes into your head without thinking about runways. Then call the tower and get a runway assignment. It'll give you good takeoff (and landing) experience in crosswinds and oblique winds, plus good taxiing practice as you try to find your way around.

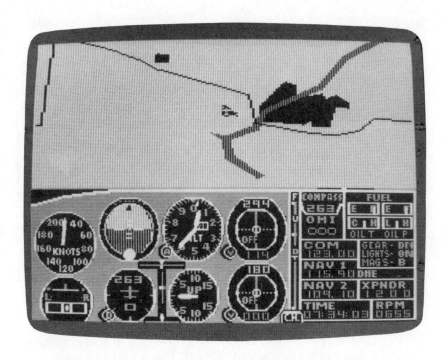

Gather by the River
Tie-Down III

North Position: 16846
East Position: 16598
Altitude: 624
Pitch: 0
Bank: 0
Heading: 263
Airspeed: 0
Throttle: 0

Rudder: 32767
Ailerons: 32767
Flaps: 0
Elevators: 32767
Time: 7:30
Season: 1—Winter
Wind: 0 Kts, 0

> Greater Kankakee (IKK), Kankakee, Illinois
> **Runways:** 4/22 (5100 × 100)—Paved,
>   centerline if in Cessna
>   16/34 (3200 × 75)—Paved,
>   centerline if in Cessna
> **Elevation:** 624
> **Tower:** 123.0
> **VOR:** Kankakee—111.6

Use radar and zoom to an altitude which puts a small, rectangular city on your screen at about ten o'clock. That's Bloomington, Illinois, about 60 nautical miles southwest of where you're tied down (shows you how far-reaching radar is sometimes).

Kankakee, of course, is the city to your right, population about 30,000. The highway crossing the entire screen is Interstate 55, which runs diagonally across the state from Chicago to the banks of the Mississippi at St. Louis, Missouri. The river behind you is the beautiful Kankakee, which was introduced in the first book of *Flight Simulator* adventures. It climbs out to the north and west and joins up with the Illinois River near Joliet. The simulator Kankakee River, however, doesn't simulate that far.

The patchwork occupying most of the left-hand portion of your screen is simply a patchwork occupying most of the left-hand portion of your screen. Maybe it's farms. Or a primitive chessboard for ancient astronauts.

Your nearest airports are Sanger to the north and, if you're flying the Piper, Dwight to the west. Dwight appears in the Microsoft manual, but like a number of other airports, it's nowhere to be found in the Cessna simulation, at least in my version. I'm missing five airports in the Chicago area alone—Bloomington, Vermilion County, Gibson City, and Paxton—in addition to Dwight.

Farthest airports are University of Illinois Willard to the south and Chicago O'Hare to the north.

The most scenic flight is in and around the city and the river themselves. Or you could go south if you want to try to find a chess partner. A daytime flight makes the most sense. At dawn, dusk, or night you won't see the river.

Choose and make one of those cross-country flights now, selecting a destination and a flight path by reference to your chart, first inserting a random surface wind, and any kind of weather you want, into the editor.

Location and taxiing information. Your tie-down is on the grass facing the taxiway. It leads to the fuel station (in the Piper you can play the fun game "Find the Fuel Pump") and to runway 4. For runway 4, you taxi ahead, take your first right, then first left, followed by a 180 to the right and the runway. For runway 22, you taxi ahead, take your first right, then another right, following the taxiway all the way to the end. Then it's a 180 to the left and the runway. Runway 34 is directly behind you. As for runway 16, just follow 34 to its opposite end, using the grass alongside the strip.

Fallout at Fallbrook

North Position: 15023
East Position: 6144
Altitude: 761
Pitch: 8
Bank: 0
Heading: 0
Airspeed: 65
Throttle: 0

Rudder: 32767
Ailerons: 32767
Flaps: 0
Elevators: 37375
Time: 15:30
Season: 2—Spring
Wind: 4 Kts, 0

On takeoff from Fallbrook Community Airpark, Fallbrook, California, your engine quits just as you retract your flaps. There is only one thing you can do to avoid nosing into the runway: *Try to make a normal landing straight ahead.*

You can land safely in both the Cessna and the Piper. But in this particular simulation, a very different technique works best for each.

Now, when you go back to have a word with the mechanic, please be pleasant.

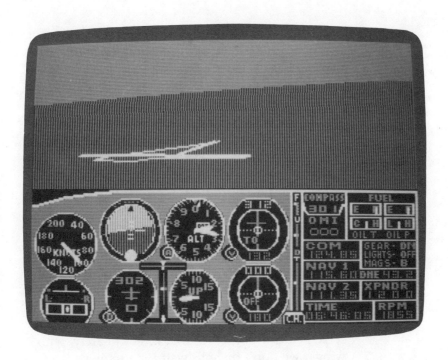

Ferry from Nantucket

North Position: 17457
East Position: 22196
Altitude: 69
Pitch: 0
Bank: 0
Heading: 330
Airspeed: 0
Throttle: 0

Rudder: 32767
Ailerons: 32767
Flaps: 0
Elevators: 32767
Time: 6:30
Season: 2—Spring
Cloud Layer 1: 12000,10000
Wind: 3 Kts, 325

This airport doesn't show up in the simulator, but it's here. In fact, you're in position for takeoff on runway 33. *Nantucket Memorial*

If you have the FAA New York sectional chart, you'll see that there are actually three airstrips here at ~~Somerset Airport~~ on Nantucket Island, which is off the southern coast of Massachusetts. On the simulator charts, the island is shown (but not identified) to the east and a bit south of Martha's Vineyard. You can see the relationship clearly on radar.

So many ships were wrecked from this storied whaling port that they built a windmill from the timbers that washed ashore. In the summer, passenger ferries operate between Nantucket and Hyannis Port to the north, and Woods Hole and New Bedford to the northwest. Fortunately, with wings, we don't have to wait for summer.

 Tune your NAV to Martha's Vineyard VOR, ~~108.2,~~ *114.5* and center the OBI needle. Then prep for your normal takeoff. Plan a left turn to fly the OMNI radial as you pass through 500 feet. Our cruise altitude will be 2300.

Roll 'em.

 You'll see Martha's Vineyard ahead as soon as you're on course. About 14 nautical miles out, the runways will come into view. Your heading takes you directly over a rather famous landmark, Chappaquiddick Island, with its equally famous bridge, right about where you make landfall.

 When the runways of Martha's Vineyard are just ahead of your nose, tune your NAV to Providence VOR, 115.6, and change your course to fly the 312 radial to that station.

The water under you is Buzzards Bay, part of Rhode Island Sound. You'll fly to the left of Woods Hole, famous for its oceanographic research, and across the coast of Massachusetts just below New Bedford.

There are several airports in the real world around Providence, Rhode Island, but they're not in the simulation. So we'll plan to land at Danielson Airport in Connecticut.

Danielson has one runway, 13/31. Since the wind is about three knots at 325 degrees, they'll be landing on 31. The runway bears on the 300-degree radial from the Providence OMNI. If we get on that radial once we're over Providence VOR, we should be almost lined up for a straight-in approach.

A few miles out of Providence, set the OBI to 300. When the reading changes to FROM, turn left to intercept that radial and center the needle.

Once you have your heading, switch to Putnam VOR, 117.4, and your DME will show you the approximate distance to Danielson, since the Putnam OMNI is nearly the same distance.

Soon, like magic, you'll see the Danielson runway ahead. And the whole exercise becomes visual.

Elevation at Danielson is 239 feet. You're at 2300 (supposedly). Remember, the runway is on a heading of 310. You'll want to get over to your left a bit to get lined up.

Back off to pattern speed and take on ten degrees of flaps as you let down. Gently. Gently.

With so much time to prepare for it, this should be one of your better landings, shouldn't it?

But two things are certain: If this is one of your better landings, there won't be a soul at Danielson to see it, and if it's one of your worst, half the population of the county will be out at the airport this nice spring morning. Watching the airplanes fly.

Reconnaissance

North Position: 17386
East Position: 7407
Altitude: 410
Pitch: 0
Bank: 0
Heading: 128
Airspeed: 0
Throttle: 0

Rudder: 32767
Ailerons: 32767
Flaps: 0
Elevators: 32767
Time: 9:00
Season: 2—Spring
Wind: 4 Kts, 55

You're on the grass alongside runway 6L, at what used to be (since this is no longer 1917) Enemy Base 2 in the simulator's WWI battle zone. Get out your illustration of the zone in the simulator manual. Enemy Base 2 is at the southern, or near, end, just east of a factory and north of a fuel depot. During the war, these were two of the numerous U.S. targets. (And isn't it amazing, that with the hundreds of thousands of pilots who dropped bombs on this zone, even just this year, not *one* target was demolished? Every one of them is still standing intact.)

Under peaceful blue skies, we're going to fly a little reconnaissance of the zone this morning in our modern aircraft. The area covers about a hundred square miles, with mountains, the river, the one-mile grid marks, and the various buildings and airstrips creating scenic interest.

 Ready your aircraft for takeoff, then taxi into position on the runway and hold.

Access radar and zoom to the view which shows you the two parallel runways, the taxiway joining them, and some of the parking area off the taxiway.

Zoom one notch higher, and you'll see that the taxiway and parking area disappear and that the two runways are represented simply by two parallel lines.

Two more notches higher (three notches in the Piper) and the southern end of the river appears, along with the western mountain ridge. Notice the fuel depot just south of your position and the factory complex at the base of the mountain. However, there's a factory missing, if our maps are to be believed. There should be a factory right off your tail, but radar doesn't reveal it. Either one factory *was* wiped out in 1917, or the camouflage is *very* clever. Maybe from the air we'll check this.

 Now return to your out-the-windshield view and take off, climbing straight out to 1000 feet. As you pass through 1000 feet, bank 30 degrees and turn right, to a heading of 180, or due south. Level off at 1500 feet at pattern airspeed.

Once level, set up a direct rear view, and keep flying on your 180 heading until the entire zone is visible behind you. Use the time to get the exact altitude, 1500, and pattern airspeed, slow flight. Take left and right rear views to get a feel for how much farther you'll be flying before the entire battle zone is in view.

Once there's some green on both sides of the battle zone scene (direct rear view), return to your forward view and turn left to fly a heading of 90 degrees. When on that heading, take a 90-degree view off your left wing tip.

Once you're opposite the point where the mountain range and the easternmost grid line come together, turn left again and head due north. The edge of the grid and the foot of the easternmost ridge of the mountain should be just about straight in front of you. They should be in a line such that you're flying along the eastern edge of the battle zone. That's our objective, so make whatever adjustments you must to get into that position. You don't have to be exactly aligned, but you should be flying pretty much along the "edge," with the eastern boundary straight ahead, and on a due north heading as you approach the zone.

When you're about three miles from the edge of the battle zone, you'll be able to check your position on radar, and once inside you can zoom one notch closer to pick up some details.

 The first things you'll observe, on radar and using your left side views, are Friendly Base 2 and its fuel depots, this side of the river. Another mile or so north is the main airbase, Friendly Base 1. As you pass this, take a 90-degree view to the left.

As the last mile marker before the mountain range slips under your nose (forward view), turn left and head 270, due west. Then, when you're over the river, turn left and track down the middle of it.

A view out the left side will show you Friendly Base 1 again, about two miles away. Quite soon, ahead and to your left, you'll spot Friendly Base 2. About the same time, famed Enemy Base 1 should be visible out the right side.

As you near the end of the river, you'll see the airport we took off from, but still no sign of the enemy factory that's supposed to be about a mile west of there.

Fly beyond the grid lines, then circle to your right around the airport and get on a north heading just this side of the mountains. A nice shallow bank should do it.

When you're opposite the airbase you just circled around, take a right side view and you'll see the Ghost Factory, very massive and real, exactly one mile this side of the runways. Out front, another factory will suddenly spring into view. If you miss it out front, take a straight-down or, ultimately, rear view. No wonder these factories were so hard to hit. They must be camouflaged with mirrors.

 Put on some flaps, and set yourself up to land on runway 4 at Enemy Base 1, just a couple of miles ahead. Squeeze over as close to the mountains as you can, because you'll need some room to make your turn for runway 4.

Once you're on the ground, take a look around. Pretty fancy base the Boche had, hmmm? But now, the whole battle zone is yours to fly around in. Use this mode as your tie-down, or the mode in Adventure 10, "Time Warps," as your starting point, and fly the whole area whenever you like. The reconnaissance will be useful, should you ever go into the World War I Ace mode on a Sunday afternoon. You just slip down the river and sneak up on the factory by...well, you know how.

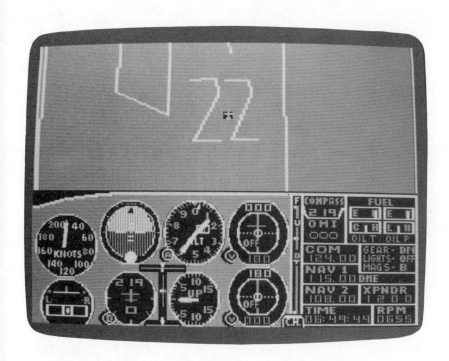

The High and Mighty

North Position: 15150
East Position: 5746
Altitude: 1601
Pitch: 0
Bank: 0
Heading: 247
Airspeed: 0
Throttle: 0

Rudder: 32767
Ailerons: 32767
Flaps: 0
Elevators: 32767
Time: 6:30
Season: 2—Spring
Wind: 6 Kts, 220

For the past five or six days I've been watching a very young budgerigar (or budgie, or parakeet) make his first attempts to fly. I knew nothing about these birds when I bought one about a week ago. In fact, I knew little or nothing about birds in general. But this little parrot has taught me a few things.

Budgerigar is the native Australian name, derived from the Australian *budgeri* 'good' and *gar* 'cockatoo' (though it isn't a cockatoo). Budgie, the Good Cockatoo.

I told the dealer I wanted the bird to be free to fly around my apartment, but it was suggested I have his wings clipped anyway for his own protection. (They'd grow back.) So they were clipped, but on my stipulation that he have wing-spread enough to at least glide. This showed great insight on my part, since the idea of gliding has never, from day one, entered Bobbie's mind. When he tries to go anywhere without visible means of support, he flaps his tiny wings madly, from start to finish. Gliding is a luxury reserved for gulls or pelicans or eagles.

Bobbie escaped from the little box I brought him home in as I was trying to slip him into his—not cage—but sleeping and eating quarters. He sort of fell, with a flurry of wings, onto the kitchen floor, then took up a huddled position in front of the dishwasher. After about an hour of coaxing, comforting, and one-sided conversation, during which he seemed sometimes to listen, he waddled to a wicker room divider I had leaning against the kitchen wall and climbed to the top of it via claws and beak. And there, about seven feet above the floor, he perched all night.

I timed Bobbie's arrival to match a week's vacation, so I could "protect" him through his early experiences in my apartment. And so we could get acquainted.

And I've become acquainted with what I regard as a sheer miracle.

I've had the privilege of watching a half-dozen first flight attempts, but, more importantly, the preparation for each of these flights. The initial flight lasted only about two seconds, and wasn't so much a flight as it was a flurry in the direction of the linoleum. He fell from the high perch to the floor in a straight line, with his wings flapping furiously all the way. Then with great dignity he stood up, walked back to the wicker room divider, and clawed and beaked his way back up to his perch.

I applauded and praised him greatly for about two minutes. I do that now every time I see him fly. Because he deserves it. I assure you, if he's any criterion, birds are not born knowing how to fly. They learn it. The hard way. What they do know is that they *should* fly. From there on out they just work at it.

Bobbie spends about ten minutes doing a preflight number on himself, physically and mentally. Between flights he spends hours, I'm convinced, planning his next.

The physical preflight is just incredible. He works with electric speed over his entire body, preening and pruning himself. The most amazing thing is that he pulls on his wings with his beak to, I believe, widen their span, literally stretch them. He also uses his claws to separate and lean

out the tail feathers, and his beak to comb and
fine-tune the scapulars, or shoulder feathers, and
the fine coverts that overlie the main wings. He
nips fluffs of surplus blue down from his breast
and white down from way in under his wings. He
bites and claws and scratches himself, and twists
around so that his head is facing opposite his
body. Then he turns on his perch and looks at the
wall and shakes all the work down, cocking his
head from side to side. He faces forward and goes
through the whole process again, biting, arrang-
ing, and rearranging each feather as if he knew
exactly what its perfect orientation was, tugging
again and always on his wings and stretching
them as far out from his body as he can. And
scratching and shaking. When he's about ready,
he chirps shrilly a couple of times (otherwise, he's
silent all day). He rehearses his flight again, the
one he's been studying for hours, with quick but
intent looks toward the top of the refrigerator, the
clear sections of the countertop, the floor, and me
(wherever I happen to be watching).

Sometimes, after he does all this, he doesn't fly.
He's just not psyched up enough. All the fervor
seems to leave him, and he slowly and quietly
slumps down and gets somnolent.

But when he flies, and each time he flies better,
it's a brief moment of rarest charm. The first few
times he just flapped to the floor. But back on his
perch, he studied the refrigerator top with an
intensity that could almost burn a hole. Not for
minutes, but for up to an hour. The top of the
refrigerator, on the other side of the kitchen from
the room divider, is his present target. He hasn't
made it yet. In his attempts, he's hit the refrigerator door a couple of times, then flapped on
down to the floor. Another day, realizing the

refrigerator was beyond his immediate capability, he decided what he needed was directional control. However, he flew to the left instead of the right to avoid smacking into the door and fell right on down into the bottom of an empty wastebasket.

But he climbed up on his perch again and studied. He thought about what he'd been doing wrong. And this morning he's begun to learn about direction. After a long preflight, he leaned far forward on his perch—his eyes bright and his whole body seeming to thin out and streamline—launched himself, and flew toward the kitchen counter next to the refrigerator. Aware when only two-thirds of the way there that he couldn't get or hold the necessary altitude, he turned right in a beautiful arc, flew a semicircle downward, and made a superb landing on the floor. This time, too, for the first time, he chirped as he walked to the divider. He was delighted with his achievement. He knew, exactly now, how to turn right to get out of trouble.

And I'm convinced a left turn will be the next study. Meanwhile, he's getting closer and closer to making it to the refrigerator top, which is about the same altitude as the wicker perch. He'll force those wings to spread. He'll just *pull* them out to where he wants them, spreading them by sheer determination. He'll lean himself out and work himself over fiercely until he has his body down where he wants it. He's going to be swift, sharp, sure. And I'm going to be a witness of it all.

I don't care if Bobbie ever talks, and says *hello* or *pretty bird* or *I love you*. Or if he learns to climb on my finger. That he flies is what matters. That's why I've given him the biggest cage I can—my entire apartment.

117

When the great American contralto, Marian Anderson, visited the mighty Finnish composer, Jean Sibelius, he greeted her with these murmured words: "I am only sorry that the roof of my house is not high enough for you."

The airport with the highest elevation in the simulator world is on Santa Catalina Island, off the coast of California. This mode gives you a convenient tie-down there, just off the taxiway at the business end of runway 22. It's yours. Permanently. Out there surrounded by ocean. Up there surrounded by sky.

Fly.

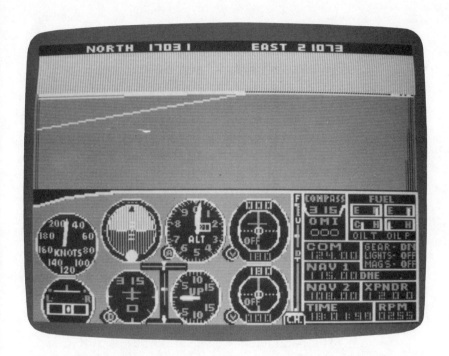

Sentimental Journey

North Position: 17031
East Position: 21073
Altitude: 12
Pitch: 0
Bank: 0
Heading: 315
Airspeed: 0
Throttle: 0

Rudder: 32767
Ailerons: 32767
Flaps: 0
Elevators: 32767
Time: 18:00
Season: 3—Summer
Wind: 4 Kts, 275

Important: Change Slew to 1 for this mode.

Follow me on this strange little trip, and you may learn a couple of things. Such as how to use slew if you haven't tried it. And mostly, how to put yourself in a place that's important to you personally, if there's any such place in the simulator world. For example, how to put yourself and your airplane in your own garage or backyard. Or how to create an airstrip that's significant in your experience, but maybe wasn't significant enough to make it into the simulator.

After we get where we're going this summer evening, I'll tell you why we went there. Or anyway, why *I* went there. I'm writing this in the act of going. In other words, I first do what I'm instructing you to do, then I write it, bit by bit. So we discover together how it all works.

The parameters we've set up put us at JFK, at the tie-down we created in an earlier adventure, but with a very small difference in heading. These will not be our final parameters. They're just a place to start. For this sort of operation we *need* a place to start.

When you exit the editor, you'll hear the engine stop and you'll see the north and east coordinates at the top of the screen. Your heading may or may not be 315. But that's the heading we want exactly.

 Open your manual to the page which illustrates slew controls, and if your heading isn't 315, use the Heading Slew keys to get on that heading.

Next, press the altitude Up slew key once (on the PC there's no up label, but it's the F2 key), and look at your altimeter. You'll be gaining altitude at 50 to 100 feet a second. (With the Piper

you'll need some more presses to get up to speed.)
Poise your finger over the Freeze or Slew Freeze
key, and press it when you show about 5000 feet
of altitude. No need to be exact.

At this point you'll see a bit of La Guardia Airport off to your right. The highway is Interstate
495. It points to and goes through the Queens-
Midtown Tunnel. That tunnel to Manhattan and
then the Lincoln Tunnel to New Jersey are straight
ahead. The blue you see is, on the near side, the
East River, and on the far side, the Hudson River.

Now tune your NAV to Kennedy VORTAC, 115.9.
Your DME will indicate that you're about a mile
from the OMNI station. To be as precise as possible, we'd like to be right over the OMNI station.
Because where we're going is exactly 28 miles
from there and on a heading of 315.

We're a little north and a little east of the OMNI
dead center, so let's first slew a little south. Press
the South key several times and watch the DME
reading. Also keep an eye on the OBI, which will
read FROM for a bit, and then at about 0.6 nautical miles will change to TO. Freeze the slew when
you have that reading.

Now press the West key a number of times, and
shortly you'll get an additional countdown. Poise a
finger over the Freeze key, and press it when the
DME reads 00.0.

How's that for precision? If it didn't work exactly for you, use your Recall key and try again.
You'll quickly nail it down.

Now we're at 5000 feet over the Kennedy
VORTAC and on the 315 radial. Next we want to

slew *ahead* exactly 28 miles. Not north, south, east, or west, but *ahead*.

To do this if you're flying Cessna, enter the editor and change the slew parameter to 2. Then exit. If your version of the simulator doesn't have the *ahead* feature, just read along until the next instruction to enter the editor, then change the parameters to those given at that point.

Pressing the North key will propel us forward on the 315 radial. You can press the key numerous times to slew faster and faster, or you can take it easy and see the lower end of Manhattan pass under you. You'll pass directly over Manhattan Bridge and the World Trade Center towers, with the Statue of Liberty over there to your left, and then across the Hudson to Weehawken.

Watch your DME as you build up distance, and ready your finger to freeze the slewing when the DME reads 28.0 nautical miles. You can slow up, remember, by pressing the South key. Do that as you near 28 to avoid whizzing right past it. But even if you passed it, simply slew south to get back. You can even slew back a tenth of a mile.

Now we're exactly over our destination, but at 5000 feet. So press the altitude Down slew key (unlabeled in the PC illustration, but it's the F10 key). You'll lose those 5000 feet in a big hurry, but you won't crash.

 One more thing we want to do here on the ground is change heading to 280 degrees, the reason for which will soon be apparent. To do this, use the left Heading Slew key, and freeze it at 280. Again, you can use the opposite key if you go past.

Now exit to the editor and you'll see the parameters of your present location. Follow down the list with me and change just what's indicated:

- Change slew to 0
- Change flaps to 0
- Change heading to 280
- On page 2, change minutes to 0

Save the mode as it now exists. The only differences are the north and east parameters and the altitude. These are now on or very close to North, 17104; East, 20881; Altitude, 410 (if you had no Ahead slew, enter these values).

Exit the editor.

Be advised: You're sitting on a piece of geography of the greatest interest to this writer. But of interest to you, too, because getting here taught you how to get to any specific place, a place that matters to *you*. It could be, as suggested earlier, virtually your own front yard. Or a farm where you spent time as a youngster. Any spot, so long as the simulator encompasses it, which is meaningful to you personally.

To determine where I wanted us to get to in this slew operation, I used a combination of tools—a map of the metropolitan New York area, showing the key routes and roads; a copy of the FAA New York sectional chart; a ruler to pinpoint what radial from Kennedy would cross the location I wanted to reach; and the same ruler to determine the nautical mileage from Kennedy VORTAC to this place.

Just what is *this place?* It's a place where a runway used to be, but is no more. You're positioned backward in time about 20 years so that you're sitting at the threshold of runway 28 at Totowa/Wayne Airport, Totowa, New Jersey, ready for takeoff. You may see only green and blue out there. I see a lovely, lonely runway in the grass, with a sunset at the end of it. And hear and feel the engine of a rented Cessna 150 out in front of me. And I run her up to 2200 rpm. I feel the flap handle in my fist as I watch the flaps come down: 10, 20, 30, 40, and back to 0. Between my thumb and forefinger I can feel the magneto switch, and then the knob of the carb heat, and see the rpm drop when the heat comes on. Everything checks out fine.

My instructor, Arnold Kufta, has just told me, "You've been safe a long time. Tonight, you're precise." He got out of the airplane a few minutes ago, back there on the tarmac in front of the office. I'm alone in this airplane. The first time that right seat's been empty. "Remember, you'll be a bit lighter without me in there. You'll climb faster."

I'll save this mode for myself, just the way we've created it. I know how to fly from here to Danbury or Westchester or Republic, or a dozen other places in the simulator, in the world it recognizes. Even though my takeoff is from somewhere it doesn't recognize. As for you, why not use this technique to create a Totowa/Wayne of your own? And let that be this mode rather than the mode set up at the start of this adventure. So you're off a few tenths of a mile in your calculations. Who'll ever know?

As for the geography you're looking at, today there are houses sitting there. And no hint of the runway I remember. But the grass—the green—in this simulator scene has some real justification. As students, we used to land on the grass instead of the runway. Easier on the tires, the airport operator said. And easier on the runway, too.

So I'll take off from the grass. And, as Arnold used to say, see the sun rise in the west.

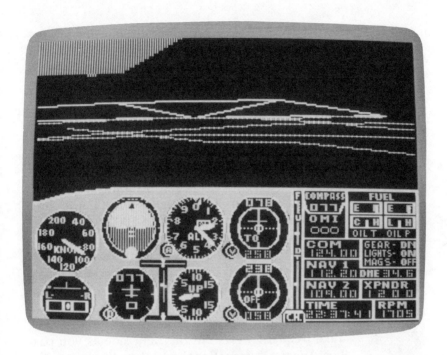

Lights Out

North Position: 15307
East Position: 5817
Altitude: 102
Pitch: 0
Bank: 0
Heading: 0
Airspeed: 0
Throttle: 0

Rudder: 32767
Ailerons: 32767
Flaps: 0
Elevators: 32767
Time: 22:18
Season: 4—Fall
Wind: 5 Kts, 310

You're poised for runway 30R at Torrance Municipal, Torrance, California. The lights ahead are those of the San Diego Freeway, Interstate 405, about four miles distant.

(If you're flying the Piper, take a look out the front left to get a better idea of the lie of the runway.)

 When you're set, taxi ahead, turn onto the runway, and continue with your takeoff. Plan to get into slow flight at an altitude of 1000 feet, and then turn right heading 317, or to whatever heading puts the tip of the coastal lights directly in front of you. You'll be just about even with the coastline, with the darkness of the Pacific spreading off to your left.

 Take frequent views out the right side as you pass Los Angeles International and then the brilliantly lit Marina Del Rey. When you're a few minutes past the marina, tune your NAV to Paradise VOR, 112.2 (if you're flying the Cessna, this station doesn't appear on your chart, but it's there and you *can* tune it).

Center the OBI needle with a TO reading, and take up the indicated heading. Admire all those lights as they swing by and under you, because you may be looking at some darkness soon.

Once you're on the radial, climb to a cruise altitude of 2500 feet and get straight and level at your normal cruising airspeed.

Take views in all directions as you fly, and enjoy the wild network of Los Angeles area highways. This is the most brilliant highway lighting display in the simulator. If you see a mountain range ahead, it's the Santa Anas.

Meanwhile, continue to correct as necessary to stay on the OMNI radial you're tracking.

As you fly further and further inland from the coast, the highways and consequently the lights, thin out until finally there's pure darkness ahead. When you have this bleak outlook, the unexpected happens.

 Chop your throttle completely. You have lost your engine.

Fine state of affairs, this. Just out on a little sightseeing trip, taking in the lights.

Well, at least you're not over a densely populated area, judging from the illumination down there. There are supposed to be a few airports somewhere around here, but in the blackness what difference does it make?

It makes a big difference. Keep a sharp eye out, all sides. If you're lucky, you'll spot a place to put her down. Maybe Chino, maybe Corona, maybe Riverside.

And maybe, if no airport's in sight, you'll just have to go down into that darkness, straight ahead, and hope for the best. Average elevation around here is 600-odd feet. Chino's 650, Corona 533. Knowing that may help a little. But you'll have to act fast. You've less than 2000 feet of altitude.

Try to put on full flaps so that you can land at as slow a speed as possible. Use radar if it'll help.

Give it your best shot. And good luck.

Sunday Driver

North Position: 17226
East Position: 21061
Altitude: 440
Pitch: 0
Bank: 0
Heading: 118
Airspeed: 0
Throttle: 0

Rudder: 32767
Ailerons: 32767
Flaps: 0
Elevators: 32767
Time: 8:12
Season: 2—Spring
Wind: 3 Kts, 150

This is runway 11 at Westchester County Airport, White Plains, New York. The airport is just this side of the southwestern tip of Connecticut. In fact, by the time you're airborne you'll be crossing the border of Westchester and Fairfield counties.

But we're not going on any nice little sightseeing trip today. You'll see some sights, sure, and from an unusual perspective. But you may be too busy to enjoy them, at least until you get where we're going.

Our destination is a secret for the moment. I want to keep you in suspense. But I will say it's important for you to follow my instructions to the letter. If things get fouled up, use Recall and try again until you get it right. Here goes.

Make your normal takeoff and climb straight out to 1000 feet. As you pass through 1000, turn right to a heading of 270 degrees. As you turn, gradually reduce your rpm to 1600–1605 and complete your climb at or close to 1500 feet. Adjust altitude as required once you're on your heading, but ultimately trim for straight and level flight at 1500 feet, with a power setting of 1600–1605 rpm, and heading 270.

The water you're flying toward is the Hudson River. The geography on the other side is more of New York State. You'll fly over the river about where the Tappan Zee Bridge crosses it, although the bridge doesn't appear in the simulation.

Keep flying straight as long as you can see water ahead of your nose. When the water disappears, turn left to a heading of 210 degrees.

Maintain your altitude within at least 50 feet of 1500. As you fly, tune your NAV to Kennedy VORTAC, 115.9. Crank your OBI around to a value of 140. That's the radial we want to intercept. The instrument will read TO. Just keep flying for now.

You're flying over the Palisades, beautiful sheer cliffs that rise above the Hudson on the New Jersey side. Before long, Manhattan begins to take shape ahead, and probably a hair to the right of your course, on Liberty Island, the Statue of Liberty.

You can visualize our operation—flying a course to intercept a specific radial of an OMNI station—as a flight over the spokes of a giant wheel lying flat on the landscape. Each spoke represents a radial, and the hub represents the OMNI station. We're looking for the spoke numbered 140, or rather, our OBI is looking for it, and will tell us when we're there by centering its needle. You can see why both instructors and books say that an OMNI radial has nothing to do with the aircraft heading. We're heading 210, but we're going to come to the 140 radial anyway. When we do, if we were to turn to that heading and fly the needle, inbound to the hub, we'd get to John F. Kennedy International Airport. But in this morning's operation, we're using the point where our flight intercepts the 140 radial as a positioning reference. We'll turn there, but not to fly the radial. Until it goes off scale, the needle will show where we are in relation to spoke number 138—left or right of it. But once we start our turn, we're no longer concerned with the radial on this particular flight.

Notice that the World Trade Center towers and the Empire State Building pop into view as we get farther down river.

When your DME reads around 14 nautical miles, the OBI needle will come on scale at the right edge of the instrument and begin moving toward center. At this point *put on carburetor heat.* This will automatically reduce your rpm and you'll start a descent. Keep a close watch on the OBI needle now, and when it moves to its center position, turn left, using a 30-degree bank, toward a heading of 167. (Now stop worrying. Would I fly you into a World Trade Center tower?)

Watch for a bridge over the East River, out there ahead of you. Point your nose toward it. As soon as you've completed your turn, put on *ten degrees of flaps,* and then—without rushing—the rest of your flaps. Start reducing your power.

Meanwhile, pay attention to that structure with the girders spanning the river. That's Manhattan Bridge. And if you could fly under it in *40 Great Flight Simulator Adventures,* you can land on it with this book. That's just what you're going to do.

Think of the bridge as a runway. It bears exactly 167 degrees. Its elevation is 437 feet. Make any and all corrections necessary to sit down very nicely on it, landing and applying your brakes as close to this end as your precision will allow.

The bridge will hold you up. It's as substantial as any runway in the simulator world. And just as straight. And plenty long enough.

Once stopped, ignore the honking of horns and the wail of police sirens and admire what you've done, from all angles. Behind you, you'll see familiar landmarks. And you'll surely be able to see some of the superstructure cables out one or several sides, as well as ahead and behind. Be sure to zoom around in radar a bit, too. Take some pictures if you brought your camera. It's not every day you land on Manhattan Bridge.

Try to explain that to New York's finest, about a dozen of whom are now thronging around your aircraft, gesturing dramatically, writing things in notebooks, and arguing with motorists to pipe down.

You have to confess to the officers that this wasn't an emergency landing, but something you did because you read it in a book somewhere. And the book didn't tell you exactly what you were going to do until it was too late.

 You convince the police that the most efficient way out of the mess is for you to take off again. They would, indeed, dearly love to see the last of you and this airplane.

It's a long bridge, and you should have plenty of room for takeoff without turning around and taxiing back. If you do need to taxi back, do that now.

Careful, however, to use virtually all the runway before you get airborne, or you could hit the cables overhead. Judge your speed along the roadway and adjust your rpms accordingly, planning to rotate only after you've cleared the last cable overhead. For a while, in other words, if you have a lot of runway, make it just a fast taxi, or hold your nose down with forward elevator pressure.

(Before you take off, don't forget about your elevator, flaps, carb heat, and anything else that may still reflect your landing configuration, or this could get serious.)

You can fly on to JFK, just off to your left, or any airport you choose. It doesn't matter where you land, because wherever you land, in the whole New York/Boston area, there'll be a gentleman from the FAA waiting, anxious to introduce himself and get to know you.

News *does* travel fast.

Tradewinds

North Position: 21219
East Position: 6343
Altitude: 204
Pitch: 0
Bank: 0
Heading: 214
Airspeed: 0
Throttle: 0

Rudder: 32767
Ailerons: 32767
Flaps: 0
Elevators: 32767
Time: 7:00
Season: 3—Summer
Wind: 0 Kts, 0

Important: Change Slew to 1 for this mode.

Check your heading when you exit the editor, and if it isn't 214, use heading Slew to correct. Call up radar to look at your position here at Olympia Airport, Olympia, Washington. Over to your right is runway 17, and at the end of the taxiway to your left is runway 26.

You can use this spot as your tie-down at Olympia, in which case change Slew back to 0 later on. For now, we're off on a special adventure.

Slew up to an altitude of 5000 feet, then slew your heading to the right to 270 degrees.

Now slew west, watching the East Position value at the top of your screen and establishing a rate of about one digit per second. Opposite slew will slow you down if you accidentally go too fast. Or you can simply freeze and restart to establish the desired rate.

The Pacific Ocean will come into view. Use radar to take a view from the highest possible altitude. Keep that radar setting, but return to your out-the-windshield observation. One thing we'll find out this morning is how much Pacific Ocean there is in the simulation.

Well, not a great deal. Everything's green again, including radar. But take my word for it, even though it's all green, it's still essentially ocean.

Increase your westward slew until you achieve a rate where the hundreds are changing about every second. Closely watch the East Position value as it approaches 0.

Now we're looking at minus values (32767 is the maximum value anywhere). Increase the westward slew to a rate where the thousands change every second or so, and watch for −32767 to go by.

Sure enough. Well before you get to East 22000, slow down so you can freeze the slew at that parameter. If you should go a few digits past it, just slew east to get back.

Now slew south at a brisk rate, but observe the North parameter carefully. Slow up soon enough to freeze on a parameter of North 18100.

Check that your North and East parameters are 18100 and 22000 respectively, that your altitude is about 5000 feet, and that your heading is 270. Then enter the editor and do only the following:

• Change slew to 0.
• Change airspeed to 125.
• Change flaps to 0.
• Change throttle to 24159 (Cessna), or 25346 (Piper).
• Exit the editor.

When you reenter the simulator, the heading may show a value other than 270. Pay no attention to your heading for the moment—everything will work out fine in the end.

It may be a good idea to have your finger poised over the Up elevator key, just in case you find your aircraft in a dive when you get back into the simulator.

Now, do these things (you have a few minutes—there should be plenty of time):

- Tune your NAV to 112.7.
- Set your COM to 119.1.
- Get straight and level at 5000, if you're not already.

Just keep flying. You'll soon be rewarded for your hard work and your patience with all kinds of neat events.

Don't read any further until at least the first thing happens. Just pay attention inside the cockpit and out the window.

What do you know about that? All happened at once. Landfall. Waterfall. Tower advisory. OBI and DME. And what was that—Logan? Then this must be Massachusetts. And you can set up a course to Logan on your OBI.

And what a flight! Westward, ho! Across the Pacific from the state of Washington. All the way westward, and around the "world." All the way across both the Pacific and the Atlantic oceans. From the capital of Washington to the capital of Massachusetts. Wow!

Having performed a feat such as that, you can now most certainly make a landing at Logan that will be a model of precision, professionalism, and unparalleled excellence.

Splendor in
the Grass
The Manhattan Project I

North Position: 17065
East Position: 20996
Altitude: 23
Pitch: 0
Bank: 0
Heading: 220
Airspeed: 0
Throttle: 0

Rudder: 32767
Ailerons: 32767
Flaps: 0
Elevators: 32767
Time: 6:30
Season: 2—Spring
Wind: 4 Kts, 220

It cost me a cool $45 million to buy the property you're sitting on. Just to create a perfect airport for you, virtually in the heart of Manhattan. This beautiful grass area, all yours, will make you the envy of every pilot in the world. In all seriousness, this is a most desirable, picturesque, and exciting private flying field for you. Give it a name, maybe your own name, or perhaps your initials, and ink it in on your chart after you understand exactly where it is. The general landing and takeoff headings (a grass field doesn't really involve specific runways) are 40 and 220 degrees. Elevation of the field is 23 feet.

Now let's get acquainted with it, on the ground and in the air.

Go into radar and zoom to the high altitude view that shows you an airport, far off to your left. That's John F. Kennedy International. Tune Kennedy VORTAC, 115.9, and your DME will tell you exactly how far you are from the airport. It's about 11.5 miles, but the exact distance varies with different computers. The highway pointing to JFK is Interstate 678, locally known as the Van Wyck Expressway. It crosses the East River as the Bronx-Whitestone Bridge, the nearer of the two bridges at about seven o'clock your position. The bridge east of that is the Throgs Neck. (A *throg* is a neutered frog.)

You can see that you're at almost the southern tip of Manhattan, with the East River to your left, Upper Bay and eventually the Atlantic Ocean directly ahead of you, and the Hudson River across Manhattan Island to your right.

Zoom in two notches, and three bridges crossing the East River become distinct, as do some Manhattan streets. The bridge far behind you is

the Queensboro Bridge, so-called because it connects the boroughs of Queens and Manhattan. Under it, invisible in the simulation, is Roosevelt
Island. The bridge continues as East 60th Street
for about six blocks, where it runs right into Central Park. The first bridge ahead of you is
Williamsburg Bridge. It continues as Delancey
Street in downtown Manhattan and joins up with
the Holland Tunnel under the Hudson River.

The farther bridge, and a superb three-
dimensional feature of the simulator, is Manhattan
Bridge, connecting Brooklyn to the Lower East
Side of New York City. Before it becomes a
bridge, it's Flatbush Avenue, Brooklyn, famed in
story and song. On the Manhattan side, it's Canal
Street, which crosses to Holland Tunnel.

The southern tip of Manhattan is known as the
Battery.

In order of their adjacency to you, the three
avenues running down the island are FDR (Frank-
lin Delano Roosevelt) Drive, Fifth Avenue, and
Broadway, the latter two bordering Central Park.
The crosstown streets are, to the north of (behind!
behind!) you, 42nd Street, and to the immediate
right of your position, well, I can't figure out what
it's supposed to be, so let's call it—at least that
portion of it this side of FDR Drive—Edge Road.
That'll be useful, because Edge Road points to the
northern boundary of your airport, and you can
use it as a landmark. However, a more important
indicator of the edge of the airport is the distinct
bend the paved metro area takes at this point.

 Exit radar and look around. Out front, crossing the
East River, is Manhattan Bridge, a great sight to
take off over (and I'm as anxious as you are). Out

the right front you can see the World Trade Center towers at Fulton Street and Avenue of the Americas. They're 110 floors high. Just visible to the left of the towers is the Statue of Liberty. Out the right rear you have a fine view of the Empire State Building at the corner of 34th Street and Fifth Avenue. Out the rear you see just a bit more of the East River, giving you a better feel for your airport. And all the left side views show you the relationship of your airport to the river.

Isn't it nice? If you happen to run into someone who's afraid to fly with you, all you have to do is sit them in the airplane and take out-the-window views. They can see every feature of the New York City simulation without leaving the ground.

Enough familiarization. Let's view your private airport from the air. (You may want to follow this flight through several times to take all the views and note all the things suggested. Take pauses as frequently as you like.)

You're pointed in the right direction. Use ten degrees of flaps, set your trim, and make your normal takeoff. Note that the (black) metropolitan area comes into view almost as soon as you're airborne.

Once you've dumped your flaps, start reducing your power to medium slow-fly the airplane (Cessna at 1605, Piper at 1650 rpm), and trim for straight and level at about 1000 feet.

What a great view of the Manhattan Bridge you have!

After you pass over the bridge (take a down view to see it pass under you), take a direct rear view of your airport, and watch until most of the bridge is visible. Then pause.

What a perfect scenic. It's about what you'll be looking at when you're on final approach in the opposite direction—heading about 40 degrees. Visualize yourself lining your nose up with the far point of the triangle, but landing just beyond the near side.

That's the Williamsburg Bridge, which you'll overfly on final when landing to the north, crossing the East River just beyond the Manhattan Bridge. And you can also see La Guardia back there beyond Queensboro Bridge. All kinds of references.

In all humility, isn't this spectacular?

 Unpause and let's fly an extended pattern to take in the whole area.

Restore your out-front view and turn crosswind (left to a 130-degree heading). You'll see JFK on the horizon when you roll out. You could be inbound for runway 13R.

Take a left rear view, and when Manhattan Bridge is about at the center of the scene, return to a front view and turn downwind (crosswind minus 90, remember, or the reciprocal of the takeoff heading). La Guardia is approximately ahead, but notice you're not in conflict with its runways.

 Take a radar view so you can get used to spotting your airport that way. In one of a couple of possible views, you'll see Manhattan Bridge as the southernmost of the three key bridges. It crosses the channel (Buttermilk Channel, it's called) at an angle, as compared to the Williamsburg Bridge just above it. And above the Williamsburg Bridge is the green strip that represents the $45 million property I've bestowed on you.

Observe the green strip on radar carefully. Remember that the actual airport lies between Edge Road, or the spot where the Manhattan metropolitan area angles out toward the East River, and the sharp point where the green strip meets Manhattan and the East River. If you land just anywhere on that long stretch of what looks like grass, you'll be likely to bump into all kinds of things and give your new airport a bad reputation.

Take various views out the left side as you fly downwind. Notice that the roads leading to the Manhattan and then Williamsburg bridges are clearly visible on the landscape—a help in pinpointing your airport lying north of them.

The road you see this side of the Empire State Building is the fabled Edge Road, so you can probably see the whole lie of your airport. If you can't, maybe you flew too long a crosswind leg, so fly it again.

(Note that the Empire State Building mysteriously vanishes now and then, often when you're about opposite it. Either that or, being quite old, it's extremely thin from certain perspectives.)

 Either now or quite soon, you'll be able to see the third key bridge, the Queensboro, and its access highway. As you come up on it, turn left to a heading of 310. (Don't confuse this with a logical spot for turning to base leg—that would be shortly after we're opposite Edge Road. We're flying an extended sightseeing pattern here.)

 You can see that the Queensboro Bridge, whatever your in-flight relationship to it, gives you another excellent visual reference for the general lie of your airport. Central Park is ahead of you, and its southern end, like the bridge, is approximately three miles north of the field.

Look out the left side down the East River toward your airport. We're not going to land this time around. But pause frequently as you fly and try to fix the scenery of the whole area in your mind. Edge Road, where Manhattan juts over toward the river. The Williamsburg and Manhattan bridges below your airport. And a little farther on, the perspectives of the three major buildings and of midtown and lower Manhattan.

 When you're opposite the second of the Trade Center towers, start a left turn to head 220 degrees, or upwind. The towers should be safely off to your left. Then look out your left side and note the now-familiar scenery from this perspective. And Edge Road, and your field below it. Then the Williamsburg followed by the Manhattan Bridge. See it all on radar, too. Fly this heading until you're beyond the tip of Manhattan and out over Lower Bay. Grab a look at Liberty, too, out the right front and then on radar.

When radar shows you're opposite the statue, turn left heading 130 degrees. Look out the left side again. You can still pick out all three key bridges and your airport. Is there a more scenic view in all the simulator world?

When the East River is under your wing tip, turn left, fly to the center of the river, and track it on a heading of 40 degrees. If you've lost or gained altitude, get yourself back to 1000.

And now observe, off to your right after you overfly Queensboro Bridge, La Guardia Airport. That's where we'll land this morning.

No, don't be impatient...everything in its own time. We'll land at your airport next time. We've only *begun* the Manhattan Project.

I am sure, your memory and/or note-making habits being what they are, that you know which La Guardia runway (of 4/22 and 13/31) is active.

And yes, a right-hand pattern is permitted.

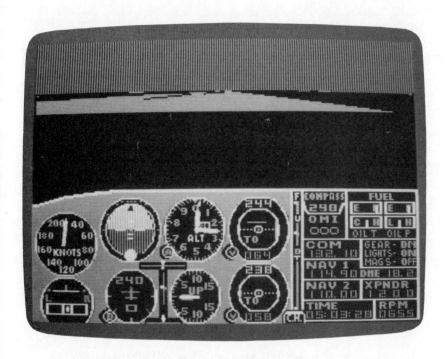

Reverse English
The Manhattan Project II

North Position: 17577
East Position: 21524
Altitude: 246
Pitch: 0
Bank: 0
Heading: 240
Airspeed: 0
Throttle: 0

Rudder: 32767
Ailerons: 32767
Flaps: 0
Elevators: 32767
Time: 5:00
Season: 3—Summer
Wind: 3 Kts, 230

Dawn at the Windham Airport, Willimantic, Connecticut, finds you on the threshold of runway 24 (6/24 is only one of three strips here). You want an early start because you've more than a hundred miles to fly. You know your destination. As promised, you're headed for your first official landing at your airport in downtown Manhattan. (If you haven't already named it, that's a name for you: Manhattan Airport.) Some friends are meeting you there for a celebration breakfast.

Now, there are many ways you could fly from Willimantic to New York City. Just find Windham on your chart, unless you're flying Cessna, in which case your chart doesn't favor you with any but a handful of major airports. For you, be advised Windham Airport is roughly 18 nautical miles northeast of Hartford OMNI.

Anyway, look at all those OMNI stations on your chart. You could map out an OMNI route easy as pie. Or three or four of them.

But this morning I'll be navigator. And I'll show you, using a single OMNI radial, not only how to fly to Manhattan, but how to fly absolutely positively straight to your new airport, as if on a homing beacon all the way.

And when we get there, I'll tell you how I worked it out, and how you can do the same for any special flight you want to make in the simulator world.

 Prior to departure, tune your NAV to Hartford, 114.9, and center the OBI needle with a TO reading. The OBI will show that you're sitting on the 262-degree radial from the Hartford VOR station. But set your OBI to 244 degrees. It'll still read TO,

and your DME will show a distance of about 18
miles. Since we want to fly across the "spokes" of
the OMNI station—say, 10–15 degrees south of
the hub, until the OBI tells us we're on the right
radial—to intercept radial 244, we'll take off and
turn right to a heading of 250. We'll fly that heading until we intercept 244, then track that radial
all the way to the strip on the East River. (If we
flew right over the hub, it wouldn't help much,
since all the radials come together there.)

 Assuming you've readied the aircraft, go ahead
and take off. Turn to head across the radials after
you have 700 feet of altitude.

With a power setting of 2105 rpm in the
Cessna, or 2050 in the Piper, trim to climb at 500
fpm to a cruise altitude of 4500 feet. We choose
this altitude because, above 3000 feet, the formal
altitude for aircraft heading between 0 and 179
degrees should be an odd number plus 500 (3500,
5500, 7500, and so on). For headings from 180 to
359, it's an even number plus 500, such as 4500
and 6500. In a general sense, these headings may
be thought of as eastward and westward
respectively.

I've written a short poem to make these regula-
tions unforgettable and dispel any possible confu-
sion once and for all:

When fly you would a heading west,
Odds are you'll evens find are best,
Plus 500.

Nice lilt to it. You might want to get it lettered
in Olde English style on parchment by a callig-
rapher and have it framed for your wall. I'd be
honored.

Although you're heading 250 degrees, your OBI is set for the 244 radial. To have some fun, set NAV 2—not 1—to tune the same Hartford VOR, 114.9, and set OBI 2 to center the needle. The OBI 2 reading will tell you what radial you're crossing at the moment. If you keep centering that needle, you'll have a steady check of the radial you're on and will be able to "see" 244 coming up. Note that each dot on the OBI scale corresponds to 2 degrees.

Don't be thrown by the fact that the radial numbers increase. You'll see that they increase faster and faster as we get closer and closer. So you'll keep pressing the key more and more often to keep the needle centered. Eventually, you'll pass zero and beyond.

When you're approximately four miles from Hartford OMNI, your OBI 1 needle will switch from off scale to center, and the indicator will read OFF. Soon after that it'll read FROM, and the needle will go off scale to the right once more, indicating the 244 FROM radial is still to your right.

The rate at which your OBI 2 needle, pointing to the station, changes indicates how close you are to that station, where the radials get closer and closer together. Note that OBI 2 still shows a TO indication. It'll continue to do that, indicating on what radial we are from moment to moment, as long as we keep the needle centered. The OBI 2 reciprocal heading, at the bottom of the instrument, steadily indicates the "from" radial. So as we get closer and closer to 244, that's indicated by the reciprocal reading. When, for example— with the OBI 2 needle centered—the OBI reciprocal reads 216, we're crossing the 216 FROM radial, when it reads 230, the 230 radial, and so on.

As we fly away from the station, the OBI 2 needle activity slows up correspondingly. Keep the needle on scale and center it frequently.

When your DME reads about 13.5 nautical miles from Hartford OMNI, note that the needle on your primary OBI creeps on scale from the right. Note, too, that the secondary OBI, when its needle is centered, confirms that you're about ten degrees from your target, the 244 radial.

As you get closer to 244, it seems like an eternity between each two-degree change of the OBI. This is because you're only six degrees off the actual radial heading, so you're roughly paralleling it. Using the spoke-and-hub analogy, you're aiming at only a slight angle toward the two hundred forty-fourth spoke. You'll thus be quite far out on its span before you actually intercept it.

We could easily correct for this by turning at a sharper angle inward in relation to the radial, thus hastening the meeting. But for the demonstration purposes of this flight, just hang in there at your 250 heading. You're flying in the direction you want to go anyway, within a few degrees.

And somewhere along the way, the sun comes up, too.

If you were approaching the 244 radial at a considerable angle, it would be a good idea to anticipate it, say, about two degrees before you get there. But since you're entering almost parallel to it, wait until your primary OBI needle is centered and then make a shallow turn to the left, subtracting just six degrees from your heading.

Notice now that your two OBIs agree. The primary OBI says you're on the 244 radial FROM Hartford to Manhattan. OBI 2 says that same radial TO Hartford is on the reciprocal heading, 64 degrees.

So what's that water out there, the Hudson River? Is this another trick? If it's the Hudson, it looks like we're flying *up* it.

But your instrument panel tells you otherwise. You're on a southwesterly course, 244 degrees, at an altitude of 4500 feet.

Go into radar and take a high altitude view, one that shows you an airport this side of the water. That airport look familiar? Now go a notch or three higher and everything jives. At your altitude you can see across the Sound to Long Island, and the Atlantic beyond it. Out the windshield you can see almost to Manhattan. The Hudson River is visible as a pencil line to the right front.

Your airport on the East River is exactly 84 nautical miles from the Hartford OMNI station (if you're flying with an Apple simulator, it's 88.1 nautical miles). I'll explain how I know that (and it wasn't by making the flight we're making now) a bit later on.

Your heading is taking you right along the north shore of Long Island Sound—a nice picturesque route.

Should be able to raise the JFK tower somewhere along here, on 119.1. Do it.

And note something interesting. Kennedy is landing on 22. Of course. Kennedy's 4/22 runways (there are two of them, left and right) agree with the landing/takeoff headings or "runways" of your airport. So anytime you don't know the weather or wind, you can check Kennedy. If they're using 4 or 22, you follow suit. If not, you can land/takeoff whichever way gives you the most favorable oncoming wind.

Soon La Guardia comes into view. You can even begin to see where the East River, rolling past the airport, swings south toward Upper Bay. Sure enough, you're in there somewhere.

You have about 4000 feet of altitude to lose between here and your airport. Our formula for start-descent distance tells us we'll want to begin our letdown about 16 nautical miles from your field. We can use that formula's information going from a VOR station as well as to it if we know how far our destination is from the station. Since 84 minus 16 equals 68, start a 500 fpm descent when your DME reads 68. But at 1000 feet, hold that altitude and establish pattern airspeed. We won't land immediately. (Again, since the Apple version distance is a bit more—88.1 to be exact— you need to start your descent at about 72 miles from Hartford.)

Our course takes us just about dead center over La Guardia's 4/22 and 13/31 runways. And you'll find we're just a little to the left of your airport, for reasons I'll explain once we're on the ground. But we're pretty precise nonetheless, after a flight of more than a hundred miles in a virtual straight line. Watch your field go by out the right side.

After radar shows you're past Manhattan Bridge, fly a big circle to the left and get downwind for a landing on runway 22 nominal, your airport. Try turning base opposite the Empire State Building.

Your friends are all watching, so make it a good one. You'll be rewarded with a celebration breakfast. If it looks like you'll mess up, go around (in which event wag your wings so you can tell them you just wanted to overfly the site as part of the celebration).

After you've celebrated, access the mode where you saved Adventure 25, "Splendor in the Grass," and I'll show you how I decided on the heading to take from Hartford OMNI, and the distance, if you haven't already figured it out.

When you exit the editor (double-check that your heading is 220), look at your DME. If you haven't detuned Hartford, you'll see that it reads 84, within a tenth or so (a bit over 88 on the Apple). So you can check the distance from an OMNI just as you check it to an OMNI, to or from anywhere in range.

Now look at the OBI. If the radial we flew— 244—is still there, you'll see that the needle is approximately centered. Approximately, but not precisely. Reset it to one radial higher, and note that it goes off-center the same distance in the opposite direction. This is because the OBI reads in increments of two degrees. So the *exact* radial your airport is on in respect to Hartford is between 244 and 246. Or 245. We flew 244 for our demo purposes, which at this distance from Hartford represents the geographical distance you observed from the air, in other words, the amount of geography you were to the left of where you are right now.

We could have flown the 245 radial, if there were such a thing, by flying with the needle held a little left of center. We'd have been closer to overflying your airport. But even then, that 245 could represent several hundreds of feet.

Anyway, you get the idea.

Headin' Uptown
The Manhattan Project III

North Position: 17065
East Position: 20996
Altitude: 23
Pitch: 0
Bank: 0
Heading: 41
Airspeed: 0
Throttle: 0

Rudder: 32767
Ailerons: 32767
Flaps: 0
Elevators: 32767
Time: 15:00
Season: 4—Fall
Cloud Layer 1: 9000,6000
Wind: 3 Kts, 35

Here's an optimum position for takeoff in the up-town direction from your grass strip on the East River.

By the way, this is as good a time as any to explain something about the elevation here. You may have an altimeter reading that's far from 23 feet. This is a simulator peculiarity—sometimes it doesn't get its altitudes correct, particularly when on the ground and not on familiar turf. Obviously, the simulator doesn't know you've turned this little green spot into an airport. Your altimeter may read in the 100's, 200's, even 500's, or more. But there's no question that you're on the ground. If you weren't, you'd fall from the sky. Obviously.

Don't worry about such elevation discrepancies. Once you land somewhere else and then fly back here, this grass will settle down to its true altitude so that when you land it'll be where it's supposed to be. Probably. I say *probably* because I can't be sure that's always the case. I've tried various tricks to make the altitude read right, but the only thing that seems to work—and that only sometimes—is landing elsewhere and returning. If you discover a better method, let me know. (Usually, once the simulator establishes that your strip is at 20 to 23 feet elevation, it remembers that as long as you fly in the area.)

 Let's find out what it's like to take off in this direction. Go ahead, but pause once you dump your flaps and admire the view ahead. How sweet it is! Every bit as interesting, graphically, as a takeoff to the south. The East River stretching ahead to your right and curving off where it passes La Guardia. Queensboro Bridge crossing your windscreen, connecting Queens and 60th Street. FDR Drive (which becomes East River

Drive north of the Queensboro Bridge), just one of a number of perspective lines meeting at the horizon. The overcast this afternoon only adds to the scene. The money I put into this great site was well spent. And you're worth every penny of it.

Unpause and continue climbing straight ahead, trimming for 500 fpm at 2105 to 2050 rpm as usual. As you reach about 1000 feet, you can see the Hudson on the other side of New York. Out to the left, Central Park. That mesh of lines to the far right is the Bronx-Whitestone/Throgs Neck bridges complex with its connecting highways. And out the right side, you see the bridges where they are, just beyond La Guardia.

 Plan to get straight and level, and in slow flight, at 2000 feet. When East River Drive disappears under your nose, turn left to a heading of 310. Then pause and look out the left side at a fine vista of Manhattan. Queensboro Bridge, again, is nearest you. The bridges crossing the bottom of the East River are the other key group of bridges. If you look closely, you can probably make out the spot where Manhattan juts over to meet the river, just this side of the Williamsburg Bridge. Right there at Edge Road.

Fly on, turning left to track down the Hudson River with the Statue of Liberty a bit to the left of your nose. Any heading that accomplishes this is fine.

Reduce your power to descend to 1000 feet for a close-up flyby of Liberty. If you aim at that portion of the New Jersey shoreline just about opposite the statue, you should be able to get fine views out the left side as you go by. You'll be just about over the New Jersey coast. When Liberty is off to your left, you may want to go into a bank for the best view.

You're going to turn and head 130 degrees here, so you'll have seen the landmark from several sides.

Heading 130, continue to keep a lookout to your left, and prepare to turn and shoot your first landing to the north. Use radar if desired to help you get your bearings and get lined up.

Don't forget carb heat and your flaps. This time and always, land as close to this end of your airport as possible, so long as you're beyond the pavement area of the city. Remember that your airport lies this side of where the pavement juts out toward the river. Also, the closer you are to the river, the more grass you have, and the more likely you are to come to a stop this side of Edge Drive, which wins you a ribbon and the gratitude of the neighborhood.

Finally, remember that your best guide to elevation here is your eyesight. You're down when your wheels say you're down, *whatever* your altimeter reads. When you're down, you're 20 to 23 feet above sea level, depending on exactly what part of the real estate you're on. If you have any doubts, look out the window.

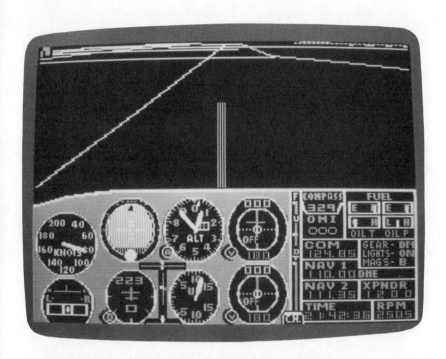

The Easement
The Manhattan Project IV

North Position: 17071
East Position: 20996
Altitude: 23
Pitch: 0
Bank: 0
Heading: 223
Airspeed: 0
Throttle: 0

Rudder: 32767
Ailerons: 32767
Flaps: 0
Elevators: 32767
Time: 21:30
Season: 3—Summer
Wind: 7 Kts, 225

This is a slightly different view of the whole situation, isn't it? Would I bestow an airport on you that offered only daylight operation? No way. So the deal I worked out includes a most important easement.

Go into radar and zoom to the view that shows your aircraft in the lower half of a rectangle (the left side of which is invisible in the Piper), and some kind of shape well off to your right. The shape, as we'll discover, is the Empire State Building.

Zoom one more notch up. Now you can see that the rectangle is a strip of pavement, marked off by FDR Drive on the left (again, invisible in the Piper), Fifth Avenue on the right, 42nd Street to the rear, and Edge Road ahead. In the Cessna, you can see where it juts out at Edge Road. So this gives you a hard surface—and a lighted—runway for nighttime operations. It's a beauty—long and wide.

But remember that the easement covers nighttime operations only. The hard surface strip is *not* to be used for daytime landings or takeoffs. If you do that, you'll get me in *big* trouble. I know I can count on you.

Let's make a takeoff now (straight ahead, you're all lined up), and as soon as you dump your flaps, set up a rear view and press the Pause key.

This is what your nighttime landing, in the opposite direction, will look like just before touchdown. In the Cessna, note how clearly the strip is lighted. In the Piper, it isn't that clear, and nighttime operation is a real challenge.

Notice how 42nd Street extends about halfway across at the far end, clearly marking the northern extremity of the runway.

Still keeping the rear view, unpause, then pause again when you see Edge Road (and simultaneously, in the Cessna, the point where the pavement juts out). This is how it'll look when you're about to cross the threshold on final approach for runway 4.

Don't be confused by the apparent shortness of the runway in this perspective. It's an optical illusion. Actually, the "runway" is much longer than you'll ever need. It looks short because the area is very much wider than an ordinary runway. When making an actual landing, you'll stay more to the right than you are now, and the perspective of the far end would terminate in the dark area to the right of the 42nd Street line. In other words, you'll be using only the right half of this paved area for landings (given that you want to execute precisely, as I'm sure you do).

Continue looking out the rear as you continue your climb-out, pausing whenever you like to get the feel of the area. Note how the line where the pavement juts out points right to the threshold of runway 4. In both the Piper and Cessna, the point is further defined, and strongly, by Edge Road. Look for Central Park. Then be sure to pause when the Empire State Building appears, and observe that it's bounded by the same crosstown streets as your nighttime strip. When you're sitting ready for takeoff on 22, you'll be able to see the grand old tower directly out the left side.

What could be neater? This mode should become your standard mode for night departures and operations from your Manhattan airport, given southerly winds. Next we'll set up a similar mode for takeoffs to the north.

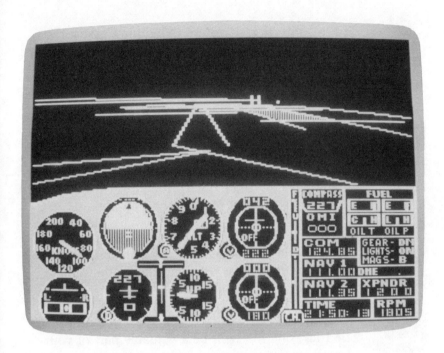

An Attraction of Opposites
The Manhattan Project V

North Position: 17068
East Position: 20995
Altitude: 23
Pitch: 0
Bank: 0
Heading: 45
Airspeed: 0
Throttle: 0

Rudder: 32767
Ailerons: 32767
Flaps: 0
Elevators: 32767
Time: 21:30
Season: 2—Spring
Wind: 3 Kts, 50

In this direction, if you're flying the Cessna, the edge of the pavement nicely defines the right side of the strip, nominally runway 4 (night) at your airport. In the Piper, radar offers a better positioning reference.

 Look at your position on radar, and you'll see that you're indeed at the end of the runway, just beyond Edge Road and where it juts out, and well situated to the right side of the pavement (which is the right side for landing, too).

Now the Empire State Building, or a portion of it, is visible out the left front. Manhattan Bridge, of course, is to your rear, and the Trade Center should be at your left rear.

 This time, after taking off, I'll show you a neat little trick, one that will be a valuable part of your repertoire.

Make your normal roll and liftoff, using ten degrees of flaps, but as soon as you dump them, slowly reduce your power to turn about 1600 to 1650 rpm.

 Take a rear view and watch for Queensboro Bridge to appear. When it does, pause for a moment and take in the scene. The horizontal line after the Queensboro, the line extending from 42nd Street, delineates the northern extremity of your airport and the threshold of runway 4 nominal. This is the picture you'll have, approximately, on final approach.

This is a good time to mention again that, on making a landing approach, your main concern should be with the runway perspective and your general surroundings, not with having or keeping an exact heading. Many runways, yours included, don't bear exactly on the runway numbers. The numbers are, after all, ten degrees apart. A runway 22 might actually point 216, 224, and so on, rather than exactly 220. And when you're making a small heading correction to line up, the literal straightness of your line in relation to the strip goes haywire anyhow. So land on the *runway*, not on its *number*.

Before you unpause, read and plan to execute the following:

- After you unpause, return to your out-the-windshield view.
- Enter the editor.
- Make this single modifictation—change your heading to 215, the exact reciprocal of your present heading.
- Exit the editor. You'll be on final approach to the runway you just left.
- Land there.

It's a downwind landing. The wind is only a few knots, though. But this is a useful trick for examining a strange airport under night conditions, or day conditions for that matter.

Remember that your most desirable landing on your night runways is to the side nearest the grass, and that side is pointed to by the extended line of 42nd Street, and indicated by the blank space between the end of that street and FDR Drive, which is at right angles. Using your eyes creatively, you can visualize a runway, the perspective of which begins where 42nd Street points and ends where Edge Road crosses your path (and in the Cessna, the Manhattan pavement juts out and ahead to join the river).

Our exploration of your Manhattan airport in this book is nearly complete. There's just one more.

But your exploration will almost surely continue as long as you fly this simulator. I think you'll come to accept your airport as a real entity, and a most convenient, picturesque, and realistic one. The nice part of it is that the people who live in the vicinity will never know the difference.

Unless, of course, *you* live there. Which, come to think of it, *is* a possibility.

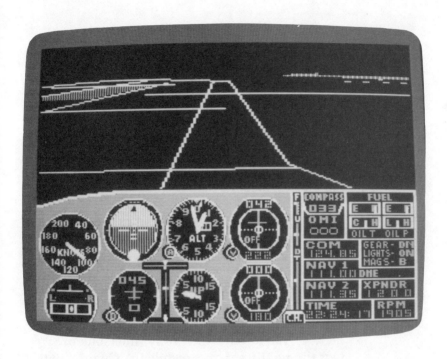

Landing
Lights
The Manhattan Project VI

North Position: 17084
East Position: 21178
Altitude: 82
Pitch: 0
Bank: 0
Heading: 11
Airspeed: 0
Throttle: 0

Rudder: 32767
Ailerons: 32767
Flaps: 0
Elevators: 32767
Time: 22:00
Season: 2—Spring
Wind: 2 Kts, 20

171

Can we successfully identify from the air, and successfully land at, your downtown Manhattan airport at night?

This mode gives you the chance to try.

We're ready for takeoff on runway 1 at Republic Airport, Farmingdale, New York, a Long Island town about 30 miles from New York City. Let's not waste time.

 Take off, climb out to 500 feet, turn left heading 280 degrees, and get straight and level at 2300 feet at your normal cruising airspeed.

As you fly, watch for JFK off to your left, a major landmark in the area, particularly at night. The highway crossing your course, pointing to Kennedy, is Van Wyck Expressway (Interstate 678). Out the right front, meanwhile, La Guardia puts in an appearance.

After the simulator accesses its disk, a bit more detail springs to life ahead.

 Look carefully. Those two lines jutting out from the general blaze of city lights. Don't they look familiar? Remember the three key bridges in our Manhattan Project, with their access highways? So where's the third bridge? Where do you think?

Take a closer look.

Yep.

Now you have a pretty good idea of where you are. That one vertical structure on the horizon must be...what's the most imposing vertical structure in Manhattan?

We took a heading of 280 from Republic. But that was arbitrary—nothing magic to it. Any reasonably westward heading would have given us a similar result. So if we'd just used our eyes in all directions, we'd have seen at least some if not all our checkpoints and had a good idea of our position.

 Remembering that your airport is north of the two downtown bridges—Manhattan and Williamsburg—see if you can't make an educated guess of its location. Maybe even see the little strip outlined on the west side of the river if you look hard enough. Point your nose to try to overfly your airport.

As you come closer, you can clearly make out, just from the lights, the two bridges and where they cross the river. You know where the river is. Manhattan Bridge, in particular, takes on its familiar reality. Can you imagine how baffling all this would be if you hadn't overflown the whole area on your last several flights and memorized your landmarks?

Don't rely on radar until you think you're over the general area of your airport. Then use radar and pause to check how accurate you were.

Accurate or not, once you're beyond Manhattan Bridge, turn left to head about 220 degrees. Since the wind is from 20 degrees, we'll plan a landing to the north, with a little crosswind from the left.

Reduce your power and get into pattern airspeed and configuration at 1000 feet.

Look behind you as you descend and see what you can identify. Looking out front, see if you can tell what's water and what's land. Use radar, too.

We'll extend the downwind leg this time, since it's your airport and you can approve a straight-in approach from wherever you please. When you have pattern airspeed at 1000 feet, do a shallow 180 to the left, and when you're heading 40–45 degrees, consider how best to get lined up for your landing.

If you're a ways out, you won't see much detail for a bit. The more or less straight line crossing your screen is the southern coast of Long Island. Use the Trade Center towers to estimate your distance. Remember, your airport is a bit north of them. And check for Kennedy to your right.

Use radar frequently to see how you're doing, and correct your course as required, remembering you still want a heading of about 40 degrees on your final approach.

Once you have a three-dimensional view of Manhattan Bridge in front of you, you're pretty well in the groove. The bridge, remember, is off to your right when you're on final to your lighted nighttime strip. You'll pass over the Williamsburg Bridge, too, before you land. Recall how everything looked out the rear view when you took off to the north.

With a bit of practice, you'll soon find this is one of the most satisfying and realistic night landings in the simulator world.

Outposts

North Position: 17191
East Position: 16671
Altitude: 591
Pitch: 0
Bank: 0
Heading: 180
Airspeed: 0
Throttle: 0

Rudder: 32767
Ailerons: 32767
Flaps: 0
Elevators: 32767
Time: 9:00
Season: 1—Winter
Wind: 0 Kts, 0

Important: Change Slew to 1 for this mode.

When we finish slewing in this mode, you can change Slew back to 0, add some kind of wind from the south, and use it as a Meigs tie-down.

Northerly Island, which is the island where Meigs is located, is so narrow that there's no other reasonable tie-down here. Add or subtract one from the East Position and you're floating in, respectively, Lake Michigan or Burnham Park Harbor.

 If, as usual, the simulator hasn't picked up on your heading as established in the editor, slew until you're looking 180–181 degrees. (Did you ever, but ever achieve a heading of exactly 180 in the Piper? If so, you're a better navigator than I am.)

That's runway 18, of course, just ahead to the right.

Go into radar and zoom to see the island and its connection to central Chicago, which is behind your airplane. The little bulge to your left rear is the site of Adler Planetarium, and there's a beach this side of that known as 12th Street Beach. A road leading to the mainland is called Achsah Bond Drive, which leads to the Field Museum of Natural History on Chicago's Lake Shore Drive. Just south of the museum is Soldier Field, home of the Bears, and to the northeast of it, Shedd Aquarium.

I've often thought how funny it will be, for those of us who know airports like Meigs only as they're represented in the simulator, to see them in reality one day. We'll expect them to be just landing strips surrounded by lots of green earth, with no people, no telephone poles, not even another airplane. We're in for future shock, I guess.

Well, I've discovered something strange in the more or less empty part of the world of the simulator—the world beyond the charts. Something—or plural, somethings—growing up or sticking up out of the everlasting grass way out in no man's land.

At slew speeds, these things are not very far from Meigs, but they're certainly far from any civilization *we* know. Come along and I'll show them to you. Maybe *you* can figure them out.

These things are to the north, so first of all, exit radar and slew to a heading of 000. Then slew up to an altitude of about 2000 feet. Next slew north, setting up a rate of about a digit per second.

In case you didn't realize it, you can pause during a slew by pressing the P key. When you unpause, the rate you've previously set up resumes. So pause for reading anytime during this journey.

You'll zip over Lake Michigan and then what must be Lake Superior at a pretty nice speed. You'll be somewhere in Ontario. There's no telling where, once you're over land. Because you're also somewhere south of Willard and all that other stuff which is far south of Meigs, though of course you're heading north. But don't be concerned.

You can look behind you and watch the somewhat familiar world recede if you want to. And you can speed up to any slew rate you like for a while. But keep a regular watch on your North Position, and when it gets to about 19150, freeze and set up a digit per second rate again. Watch straight ahead out your windshield.

When you see what appears to be a pair of dots straight ahead, freeze the slew. Then start it up again, noting that the dots don't seem to change aspect for quite a while. They must be very far away indeed.

Control the slew rate now so as to approach the dots at a brisk speed, but not so fast as to pass them right by. When North Position is in the 19900's, the dots will start to be animated. They'll take on various shapes, independent of one another, from fat to flat.

 Attention! When the dots start to move quite rapidly toward you from their position close to the horizon and begin to spread apart, freeze again.

Now slew so that the dots approach you slowly.

Before the first of the right pair of dots, which now appear to be posts, leaves your field of view, freeze again.

Study the right pair a moment. The left grouping apparently consists of many more, but similar, posts. We'll examine them more closely.

Slew west now, at a not too rapid rate, until the main group of posts is in the center of your screen. Then freeze.

Take a look out the right front. The two posts we're leaving in favor of a closer examination of the cluster are there where we'd expect them to be. They are, certainly, things of substance.

Return to your front view. Again slew north cautiously, freezing before the nearest of the posts goes out of your field of view.

Slew you altitude now to descend to the ground, if ground this is.

There the posts are—ahead of you, fat and real, arranged in a not quite orderly rank or file. Take a view to the right rear to check on the earlier two posts. There they are. Return to the out-front view.

Now slew forward slowly, right toward the posts.

They *are* posts aren't they? But what kind of posts? Guideposts? Listening posts? Outposts? Last outposts?

At least one of them will be directly in your path. Continue forward and see if your aircraft will knock them down, or they'll crumple your wings or fuselage. Watch them go by you, marching like stilted wooden soldiers.

And if you think you don't pass right through them, or they through you, look out the rear and see them align themselves behind you. When you've passed the last of them, slew around to head 180 or thereabouts. There they are again.

Slew south now to approach them from this side, and slew east or west to get one of them directly ahead of you—close up and right off your nose.

Seems to vanish inside the plane, or inside something, doesn't it? You can't actually make contact. Slew very slowly in the opposite direction, and it appears again, like a Jack in the Beanstalk vine.

If you're flying the Cessna, there's just one more anomaly way up here in northern Canada. Go into the editor and change the time to 23:00.

Aha! No posts. And also no darkness.

But look at your wings and your fin. That's where the darkness went, perhaps. Shades of the twilight zone we explored in the first of these books.

Go back into the editor and change the time to 12:00. We'll get the posts back, so we can study them some more.

I said, get the posts back, so we can...

I said, get the posts....

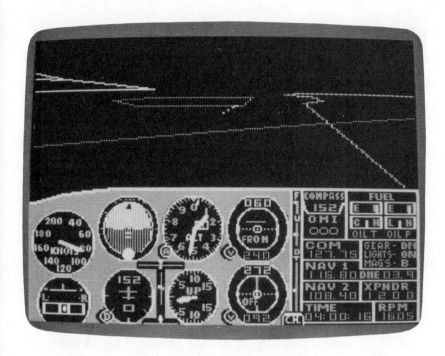

The Auburn Abstraction

North Position: 21314
East Position: 6593
Altitude: 1529
Pitch: 359 (IBM only)
Pitch: 358 (all except IBM)
Bank: 0
Heading: 152
Airspeed: 96 (IBM only)
Airspeed: 119 (all except IBM)
Throttle: 14335 (IBM only)

Throttle: 16383 (all except IBM)
Rudder: 32767
Ailerons: 32767
Flaps: 0
Elevators: 35583 (IBM only)
Elevators: 36607 (all except IBM)
Time: 4:00
Season: 2—Spring
Wind: 12 Kts, 155

I'm sure Bruce Artwick didn't set out to paint such abstractions as this, but the simulator world at night—like the world itself at night—offers many of them. Pause and admire this one. It's composed of nothing more complex than a couple of metropolitan areas (the southern outskirts of Seattle in the foreground, and Auburn, south of Auburn Municipal, beyond the airport), Interstate 5 going south on your right, and the western slope of Mount Rainier on the horizon. (Unfortunately, the metropolitan area outlines and brilliant colors are not visible in the Piper version. If you're flying the Piper, this isn't exactly a painting you'd put on your wall.)

Another nice thing about the picture is that you're cleared for a straight-in approach to runway 16 at Auburn Municipal. Being 4:00 a.m., there isn't much traffic around. Take over and fly it. You'll want to get over to your left and put some flaps on. Don't forget carburetor heat. Elevation here is 63 feet.

Long approaches at slow speed can be beautiful at night. Once you're lined up, everything seems suspended. Because the world is asleep, your engine obliges by being quieter.

Of course, you can't appreciate the suspended feeling, the silence of the hour, or the quality of the painting if you're weaving wildly all over the sky trying to get into position. And the only cure for that is to learn to draw straight lines.

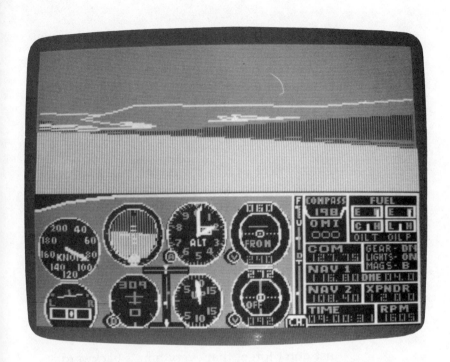

Which Way
Is Up?

North Position: 21308
East Position: 6588
Altitude: 2000
Pitch: 7
Bank: 177
Heading: 314
Airspeed: 106 (IBM only)
Airspeed: 123 (all except IBM)
Throttle: 14335 (IBM only)

Throttle: 16383 (all except IBM)
Rudder: 32767
Ailerons: 32767
Flaps: 0
Elevators: 18943 (IBM only)
Elevators: 27647 (all except IBM)
Time: 9:00
Season: 3—Summer
Wind: 6 Kts, 315

Note: The fuel starvation described here occurs only in Cessna.

What kind of weird sky and what kind of crazy landscape is this? I'm not so sure I relish flying with you after all. Some of your antics are really questionable.

Okay, you're upside down. You might as well just hang in there. Give me some time to think. The longer you hang here the better.

I knew it! I knew it! The engine quit. How do you expect gravity to feed fuel to the engine if the fuel's lower than the engine?

I expect you to get me safely on the ground at Snohomish. Right side up.

Just don't forget that everything's backward now. To see more sky, you have to put your nose down and vice versa.

Throttle won't do you any good when there's no engine, my friend. And the only way to get your engine back is to put the horizon back where it belongs. I don't care what you do or how you do it. But do *something!*

Who, me? Don't ask *me* how to get out of this situation. *You're* the one who's in the left seat. *You're* supposed to be flying the airplane.

In fact, I don't have to stay in this airplane at all. And I'm not. I'm leaving. Now. Exactly the way I came. I'm exiting the word processor and the whole deal. *Right here.*

Speaking of hanging, once you get the hang of this, you can test yourself and see how long you can stay upside down. Crackups, of course, disqualify a try. Check your clock at the outset, then check it again when you turn right side up. See if you can keep beating your own record.

Maybe you should start a competition with your simulator friends. Organize a club. Design buttons and get yourselves some T-shirts. Create stickers for your car windows. Publish a club newsletter. Have little "Upside-Downer" outings and picnics. Maybe get a baseball team going. Get your local newspaper to do an article. There are all kinds of neat things you can do with your new club.

If that's how you think, then count me out!

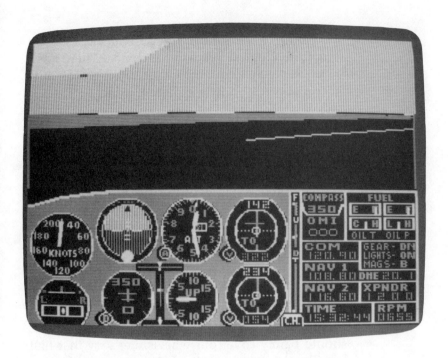

A Fine Fleecing

North Position: 17358
East Position: 21123
Altitude: 460
Pitch: 0
Bank: 0
Heading: 350
Airspeed: 0
Throttle: 0

Rudder: 32767
Ailerons: 32767
Flaps: 0
Elevators: 32767
Time: 15:30
Season: 3—Summer
Wind: 4 Kts, 35

Everything in the simulator is so realistic, I can't accept the illogical behavior of clouds. There has to be *some* way to get the editor to act reasonably on this subject. So let's explore it a bit.

You're in position for takeoff on runway 35 at Danbury Municipal, Danbury, Connecticut. There are, as you can see, no clouds.

Now follow along with me:

Go into the editor. Note that the altitude reading is 460. That's the elevation at this particular spot on runway 35. (Elevations don't always agree with what the instruction manual says, as you've probably discovered.)

Now, if we set up a one-foot high cloud here, it should barely cover our wheels. Let's try that first. Set Cloud Layer 1 tops to 461, bottoms to 460. Then exit the editor.

We're sitting in a nice little fleecy cloud. We can see the blue sky. Out the side, in the Cessna, we can see sky under our wings. In the Piper, our wing is obscured in the cloud. And out the back— well, out the back we can see the top of our fin in the Cessna, but not in the Piper. But even in the Cessna, wouldn't you expect to see more fin than that with cloud tops only one foot off the ground?

Let's see if we set both tops and bottoms to the runway elevation, 460. Go into the editor, type in the change, and exit to the simulation again.

Apparently, there's no such thing as a fractional, say, 3/60 inch, cloud in the simulator.

Let's find out what the minimum thickness is.

As long as, in the Cessna, we keep seeing our fin, we're at or under the minimum.

Go into the editor, set Cloud Layer 1 to 465 and 460, then exit again. In the Cessna we still see fin.

Go in and set 470 and 460 if you're flying the Cessna, 473 and 460 if you're flying the Piper, then exit.

Wipeout. No fin, no wing, no sky.

Go back and set 469 and 460 for the Cessna, or 472 and 460 for the Piper, then exit again.

Okay. The thinnest cloud layer we can set up is 10 feet thick in the Cessna or 12 feet thick in the Piper from its tops to its bottoms. This means if we take off in a total overcast, we'll go from no visibility to blue sky as soon as we have 10–12 feet of altitude.

Let's check that out. Go into the editor, set clouds at 470 and 460 for the Cessna or 473 and 460 for the Piper, then exit. You're all lined up, so make a normal takeoff.

As soon as you're satisfied that the cloud layer was indeed just about 10 feet thick, press the re-call key. Unless you inadvertently saved one of the cloud modes, you'll be back on runway 35 with a clear day.

Let's try something else. Set the tops to the field elevation and the bottoms 12 feet underground. (Well, they won't really be underground, just below our present elevation.) Enter the editor and set Cloud Layer 1 tops to 460 and bottoms to 448.

Which proves nothing.

So let's try putting the entire 12-foot-thick layer below our elevation. Enter the editor, set 454 and 442 for Cloud Layer 1, and exit.

Now wouldn't that jar you? We're looking right through the ground at the cloud layer. And it's six feet under.

So if six feet isn't enough, let's try our magic number. We'll use 13 to accommodate those of you who're in the Piper. The 12 for one thickness of cloud, and one more for good measure.

Go in. Set 447 tops, 434 bottoms. Go out.

Now I ask you—is that reasonable?

There's got to be some cloud level that we won't see right out our windshield here at 460 feet above sea level.

Let's be dramatic. Go in and set tops at 13 and bottoms at 0. Exit.

Okay. The simulator knows we're at an elevation above the tops of Cloud Layer 1. But does it still know there's a Cloud Layer 1?

Let's get a weather report and find out. Tune your COM to Sikorsky, 120.9. Hmmph! No mention of overcast.

Well, Sikorsky's elevation is 10 feet MSL. They should see those tops at 13, shouldn't they?

Let's give them a break and raise the cloud a bit. Well above their elevation, but well below ours—far enough, in other words, so we can't see the weather from here.

Sock in Sikorsky with bottoms at their elevation, 10, and tops at 20. Go into the editor and set it up—tops 20 and bottoms 10. Then exit.

Well, now, that's not fair!

We've got to find the minimum ceiling that won't put us in this cloud. That's obvious. We know that 13,0 gives us no cloud here at Danbury. And if somebody on the runway at Sikorski has cloud, we can't prove it from the weather they're broadcasting.

Let's try 25,0. Go in, do it, go out.

Aha! So far, so good. Check Sikorski.

Nope.

Try 100,0. They ought to recognize an overcast at that altitude.

Maybe the zero bottom is what's fouling us up. Try 100,20.

So that puts us back in the cloud again.

Is there a solution to this?

Let's go briefly to Sikorski and see if we can set up an overcast there that the tower recognizes—a minimum overcast. Then come back here to Danbury and see what gives.

Go into the editor and change North Position to 17287, East to 21249, and Altitude to 10. Set zeros on all cloud layers. Don't save this, but just exit with these parameters in place.

Now we see a clear day. So go back in and set up that 13,0 for Cloud Layer 1. We know it gives us no cloud at Danbury; so what about here at Sikorski? Exit and see.

No good. No cloud.

Try 13,1. Maybe the zero is the misnomer.

So try 13,10.

Well, that puts us in a cloud, with blue sky visible. But call the tower and you'll see they don't know the runway is shrouded in a three-foot-high overcast. Could anybody land in this?

Let's see what this 13,10 does to us back at Danbury. Go into the editor and change North to 17358, East to 21123, and Altitude to 460. Check that Cloud Layer 1 is 13,10, and if it isn't, change it. Then exit the editor.

So here we are sitting in the middle of a three-foot-high cloud whose tops are at 13 feet above sea level, all of which is fine. But we're in an airplane sitting on a runway which is a measured 460 feet above sea level. And supposedly there's solid ground under our wheels.

There's only one solution to this. Call the tower and demand an explanation!

Anyway, you can use this mode as a quick departure mode from Danbury's runway 35. Or you can use it as the basis for a lifetime study of cloud formations in the *Flight Simulator*. All you'll need is a staff of about 150 assistants all setting random tops and bottoms 16 hours a day for the next 16 years.

The outcome is clear.

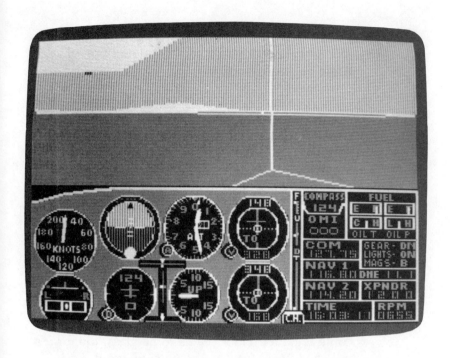

Avionics
Package

North Position: 21416
East Position: 6595
Altitude: 460
Pitch: 0
Bank: 0
Heading: 190
Airspeed: 0
Throttle: 0

Rudder: 32767
Ailerons: 32767
Flaps: 0
Elevators: 32767
Time: 16:00
Season: 2—Spring
Wind: 0 Kts, 0

Add for this mode: Sound 0.

It isn't every day you find yourself in a situation like this. Now, if you could just figure out what situation you're in....

Take a look out all sides of the airplane.

You're sure inside something. Unless you're looking at the bottoms of some giant mike stands. Maybe you just flew around the world, and there's a crowd here to greet you, and you'll be on the six o'clock news. But there are no cameras out there.

Just water. And ground. And some mountains. And those strange corners of something.

Analyze it—there's a corner ahead of you, where two things, panes of glass or something, come together. Floor seems to be glass, too, or it's matched beautifully to the outside world. So if there's a corner ahead of you and you're in a box, then there should be a corner behind you. Take another look.

Nothing. There's a corner at the right rear, if it *is* a corner, but that doesn't match the one ahead of you.

Try the left side. Another corner. What kind of shape does that add up to?

Try radar. And zoom in and out a bit. Some kind of big circular thing, like a smoke stack. Or a black hole.

You're sitting there like a bit of fuzz at the bottom of a tall, collapsible cup. And when you zoom around, you can see what kind of shape the section you're sitting in has. That explains the views out the windows.

So it's a roundish thing bottoming out in a triangle. With you in an airplane on the floor of it.
And it's transparent from top to bottom. Seems
like it must be a package.

And it is. You're a toy pilot in a toy airplane,
and you're in a transparent plastic gift wrap.
That's why it's so quiet.

 Now return to the out-front view, and set your
flaps and trim for takeoff. Add full throttle and
you'll see yourself be torn excitedly from the
package by a happy youngster. Make your normal
takeoff, and take a look back. You can still see the
tall circular package, standing right up there. Keep
looking back. What a tall package! And tied with
two bows at the top.

The lucky youngster is pretending to fly you,
and you're carried higher and higher until, when
your toy altimeter reads 1000 feet, that's as high
as the youngster's arm can reach. So cut your
power completely, still looking out the rear. Then
look out the front. See how smoothly the young
pilot brings you back toward earth. Or is it toward
that blue pool in the backyard?

Well, either the young hand lost its grip, or
you've been deliberately and maliciously set up
for a violent argument with gravity.

Which you lose, obviously.

After which, you're placed back in the wrap
while other packages get opened. Meanwhile hope
the sun will dry you off.

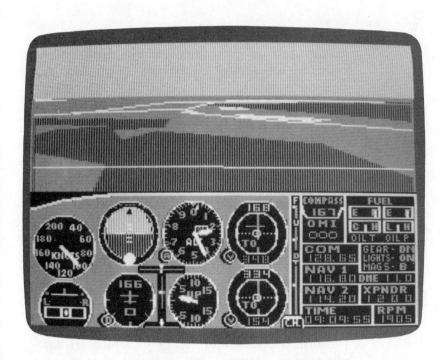

In Search of
the Floating
Bridges

North Position: 21481
East Position: 6738
Altitude: 50
Pitch: 0
Bank: 0
Heading: 250
Airspeed: 0
Throttle: 0

Rudder: 32767
Ailerons: 32767
Flaps: 0
Elevators: 32767
Time: 9:00
Season: 4—Fall
Wind: 5 Kts, 245

There's this body of water called Lake Washington on the east side of Seattle. And there's this island called Mercer Island in the center of the lake. And there are supposed to be these "Lake Washington floating bridges," which are a tourist attraction. And the Piper version of the simulator even claims, as one of its interesting topical features, "Mercer Island and Evergreen Point Floating Bridges."

As far as I can remember, I've never seen a floating bridge. Also, I've never been to the state of Washington, let alone to Seattle, except in the simulator.

So I would like to find these floating bridges and see them up close. Although I've flown frequently in the Seattle area and noted a few bridges crossing water here and there, they looked like just ordinary simulator "bridges," which are simply ordinary highway lines crossing bodies of water.

This morning, you be the pilot and I'll be the navigator as we try to find any bridge over Lake Washington which is more than a highway-type pencil line.

As far as I can tell, there are just three bridges which have anything to do with Lake Washington. One is a few miles north of Mercer Island and connects Bellevue, Washington, to central Seattle. The other two connect Bellevue to Mercer Island and then Mercer Island to, again, central Seattle.

 We're looking out at runway 25, Flying F Ranch Airport, Monroe, Washington. Tune your NAV to Seattle VORTAC, 116.8, so we'll have an idea how far we are from the Seattle area. However, we won't fly there in a straight line. Instead, we'll fly west a bit and then point south.

Take off normally, but get level and in slow flight at 1000 feet. We'll want to do some close-up observing, and I forgot my binoculars.

Keep your takeoff heading for a bit. That's Harvey Field off to your right, and presently the strip at Martha Lake Airport will appear on your left. Snohomish County is the big airport beyond and to the right.

The highway on the other side of Martha Lake is Interstate 5. Turn and track it south as you come up on the airport.

Follow I-5 where it bends westward, but keep the highway a bit to your right. Presently, you'll be able to see the northern banks of Lake Washington up ahead. Aim for the center of the lake. You'll be able to see where you are very clearly on radar.

Don't turn where the lake bends left, but stay straight on your course. You'll be flying over a little nub named Sand Point. When you can make out the northernmost of the bridges crossing the lake, turn left a little to fly across its approximate center.

Pause whenever and wherever you like to examine the bridge closely, from all possible angles. Does it look like it's floating? Or does it just look like any other simulator bridge crossing a highway.

I vote this first bridge no candidate for a floater. So if there are floating bridges (plural), then they must be the two bridges still ahead of us.

Take a close-up radar view that shows Mercer Island and the two bridges connecting it to Seattle on the right and Bellevue on the left. Then turn right to overfly the approximate center of the one crossing from Seattle.

Again, examine this bridge closely for signs that it's floating. When you can't see it out front anymore, look down and watch it pass under you.

Did you see it?

Now fly counterclockwise around Mercer Island, and then north to inspect the other bridge, to Bellevue, again overflying its approximate center.

Well, they're nice bridges, aren't they? And Lake Washington is a very attractive lake. But if those bridges can float, then so can all the other bridges in the simulator.

Except, of course, that stalwart bridge by your airport in downtown Manhattan, the airport for which I floated that multimillion dollar loan. And I haven't even got a thank you note.

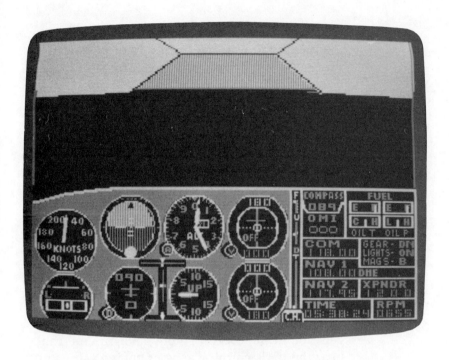

Dawn Patrol

North Position: 17418
East Position: 7448
Altitude: 410
Pitch: 0
Bank: 0
Heading: 180
Airspeed: 0
Throttle: 0

Rudder: 32767
Ailerons: 32767
Flaps: 0
Elevators: 32767
Time: 5:30
Season: 3—Summer
Wind: 6 Kts, 267

No library of tie-downs would be complete without one at the wartime base in Europe, now an up-to-date airport where you can fly your modern Cessna or Piper.

I tried to put you right in the hangar, but it can't be done. Remember, there's a significant distance between position parameters. You can taxi to an exact position. But that doesn't mean you can fix that position exactly, once and for all, in the editor. It takes some experimenting with North and East parameters to pick an optimum position on any airport.

But this one in Europe is probably better than a spot right in the hangar. Because you're ready to go at a moment's notice, parked just off the threshold of runway 27. The hour—5:30 a.m.—gets you in the cockpit before daylight. You can hear the birds chirping as your engine warms up.

I regard this airport, accessed this way with all your equipment functioning, as the one airport in the simulator where *anything* goes. In fact, the whole Europe 1917 setting is such an area, but this is your base.

There are distinct advantages to runway 27. You have a scenic takeoff over the river and toward the mountains. But more important, you have a three-dimensional reference—the hangar—when you're shooting landings. The lack of such references at simulator airports is one of the reasons landings are so difficult. Almost anything vertical—a tree, telephone pole, car, or person standing near the runway, or better yet, a couple of airplanes on the ground—would help us visualize our relationship to the airport area and the runway in particular. Maybe future versions of the simulator will provide some of these.

Meanwhile, the runway you're looking out at makes for great approaches from both directions. And it's plenty long enough for touch and go.

I talked about anything goes just a moment ago. By that, I mean doing any and all the things you might hesitate to do at a busier and more formal airport. Buzzing the hangar or flying a few feet above the strip at high speed or stunting at low altitudes, doing rolls on takeoff, or whatever comes to mind.

Further, you have other great airstrips to fly to in the area, with a variety of runways and plenty of challenges—approaches to the runways of what was Enemy Base 1 in WWI, where you have mountains to contend with, for instance.

 Take off and fly the pattern here a few times, practicing touch and go, and getting familiar with all the visual references on each leg. The next adventure will provide you with essential data for all the airports in the area, so you can expand your horizons and fly with fine precision.

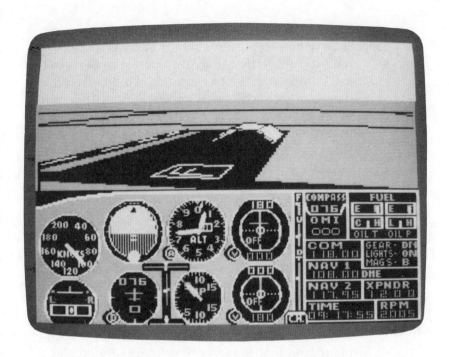

Red Quiver
Valley

North Position: 17416
East Position: 7404
Altitude: 410
Pitch: 0
Bank: 0
Heading: 180
Airspeed: 0
Throttle: 0

Rudder: 32767
Ailerons: 32767
Flaps: 0
Elevators: 32767
Time: 9:00
Season: 2—Spring
Wind: 4 Kts, 270

Soldiers in all wars have had a habit of applying code names to places where they lived and fought. And fought to live. What we've been calling Europe 1917 is no exception. I'll give you the names of all such places for the Europe 1917 sector so that you can fly by them hereafter. For no immediately obvious reason, all these names are American Indian–style names.

Of course, you can forgo these and use your own. But I assure you that, if you do, no one will have the foggiest idea where you're talking about.

Along with the names, I'll give you other pertinent data that will help you fly hereabouts.

Get out your manual and turn to the map of the WWI Ace battleground. The entire ten-square-mile area is called Red Quiver Valley. This for the simple reason that the river which virtually divides it has the fanciful name Red Quiver River (possibly because many a pilot was quivering as he flew across it into enemy territory).

Clockwise, beginning with the WWI Main Base in the upper right-hand (northeastern) corner, here are the names of the airports and the numbers for their runways:

Eagle Field (originally Main Base, or Friendly
   Base, 1)
Named for its shaky resemblance to an eagle as
   seen from the air.
Runways: 9/27, 15/33
Elevation: 410

Axe Handle (originally Airbase, or Friendly Base, 2)
Named for appearance similar to hatchet or axe as
   seen from the air. The handle is the runway.
Runway: 11/29 (nominal)
Elevation: 400

Quiver City (originally Enemy Base 2)
Named for its proximity to Red Quiver River and
its supposed similarity to a quiver when seen
from the air.
Runways: 6L/24R, 6R/24L
Elevation: 400

Wigwam (originally Enemy Base 1)
Named for its shape, obviously.
Runways: 4/22, 9/27, 15/33
Elevation: 400

*Note that elevations are inexact, and may vary from
400 to 425.*

(Earlier modes in this book have placed your
aircraft on some of these airports. You may want
to go back and pencil in their new names.)

The mountains marking the western boundary
of the area were all in enemy territory and are
collectively nicknamed Bad Bulges. The range to
the north was half on enemy and half on friendly
territory. East of the river they're called the Happy
Hills, and west of the river, Trappers Alps.

The once-enemy factories also have names,
relating to their locations in respect to Wigwam,
the former main enemy base. They're simply
called Wigwam North, Wigwam West, and Wigwam South.

You're looking across runway 33 toward runway
27 at Wigwam. Prepare for takeoff and taxi ahead,
turning onto 27 and accelerating for your takeoff
roll.

Use all your rpm and climb straight out on the
runway heading until your altimeter reads 1000
feet. Then make a 60- or 70-degree right turn and

head north toward the Alps. If you made a good normal takeoff, this should pose no problems.

Transition to pattern speed, straight and level at 2000 feet. Check radar. There should be a good half mile between you and the Bulges on your left.

When the last mile marker disappears under your nose, turn right and head due east toward Red Quiver River. Enroute, reduce your power and descend to 1400 feet.

When the river just about divides your windshield, turn right heading 150 degrees and adjust if necessary for 1400 MSL. You'll see Eagle Field ahead to your left, and you'll be downwind for runway 33, with a slight crosswind from 270 on final.

Enjoy many flights in Red Quiver Valley. It's one of the most realistic and graphically satisfying flying areas the simulator offers.

Thataway

North Position: 21347
East Position: 6312
Altitude: 279
Pitch: 0
Bank: 0
Heading: 0
Airspeed: 0
Throttle: 0

Rudder: 32767
Ailerons: 32767
Flaps: 0
Elevators: 32767
Time: 14:00
Season: 4—Fall
Wind: 5 Kts, 345

My first and favorite instructor, Arnold Kufta, at the then Totowa-Wayne in New Jersey, was an old-timer who had very little patience with protracted flight planning. He said it was okay to sit down at a desk with all kinds of slide rules and calculators and charts and meticulously work out a course "if you're not going to go." But if you *were* going to go, he believed, you should get in the airplane and start off. No further ado.

We were standing out in front of the hangar one summer evening, and he looked at me and said, "Which way is Danbury?"

Instinctively I pointed sort of at the sky and sort of to the northeast, and said, "That way."

"Okay," he answered. "So let's go."

The idea was you get in the airplane and take off, and when you get out of the pattern, you turn in the direction you know your destination lies. And *then* you start doing what you have to do to be accurate. It wasn't that he didn't believe in flight aids. He just believed that the place to use them was in the air and on the way. "If you ever fly for hire," he'd say, "the passengers aren't going to wait while you sit down at a desk and work everything out. They'll find a pilot who's ready to go right away, not an hour from now."

 So you're looking through your windshield at runway 35, Sanderson Field, Shelton, Washington. And your destination is Harvey Field in Snohomish, which is sort of in the sky and sort of to the northeast. Thataway. Let's get going.

When you're straight and level at 3500 feet, pointed toward Harvey, look at your Piper version of the Seattle chart (reproduced here and included as part of the appendix, courtesy of SubLogic Corporation, for the benefit of Cessna pilots, whose charts do not show the smaller airports).

Eyeball a straight line from Sanderson Field to Harvey Field. Look at the bodies of water along the route and particularly at the airports you can use as checkpoints. They're more reliable than water, especially in the simulator. So now you know what to look for on the ground.

Keep a continuing watch out all your windows. Make outside checks as regularly as you make instrument scans. If things don't look right, keep looking until you understand what's wrong with the way they look, then make the corrections your new information calls for. Bank and turn the airplane as necessary to point it where it's supposed to be pointed.

Don't start worrying if you feel you're lost. You have a full tank of fuel, clear weather, a chart, and a pair of eyes. You know exactly where you're going. It's a simple matter of looking and thinking. That's called contact flying.

The simulator is tougher on this type of flight than is the real world. Some simulator airports, for example, don't show up right away. But then, some airports seem to be awfully difficult to spot from the air in real flying, too.

Don't turn to new headings aimlessly. Wait until you have a pretty good idea where you are, and then get where you're supposed to be. Use radar if it helps. Use anything except your NAV system. (You're in a rented airplane that doesn't have one.)

After all, you're a bit familiar with this whole area just from flying various modes in this book.

211

Note on the chart how many runways a given airport has, and which way they point, and what if anything they're near, like water.

And look out your windows!

When you get over Puget Sound, note that you can consider Harvey Field's location with reference to at least three other airports: Snohomish County, Martha Lake, and Flying F Ranch. And note how useful (particularly if you're flying the Cessna) the FAA sectional charts would be when you're flying the simulator. They show, of course, more detail than even the Piper charts.

Snohomish, being a major (favored) airport in the simulation, will be the most prominent in both your radar and out-the-windshield views.

So if you find you aren't flying straight arrow to your destination, you'll still get there much faster than by doing all that desk work Arnold used to argue against. And certainly, if you were to use your radio stack, you could have picked up your heading after you got airborne, using Paine VOR (given that, if flying the sparse Cessna charts, you knew where Harvey Field was).

Coming near your destination, don't fail to note that little finger of water pointing up to Snohomish. Its name is Washington Lake, and we flew down it a few modes back, checking on the fabled floating bridges. Remember? Its purpose here is to help you point at Harvey Field.

The runway at Harvey bears 14/32. So remembering the wind, you'll know which end is active.

Isn't this an exciting and challenging way to fly?

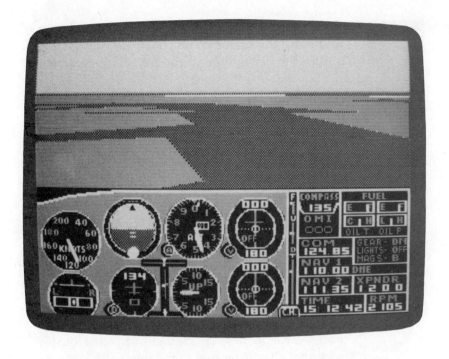

Admire the
Scenery

This final adventure in the present group introduces a new
and breathtaking concept in simulator flying: *Scenery Disk*s
from SubLogic, which ultimately will cover the entire conti-
nental United States. The following flight requires you to have
Scenery Disk 1, which should be readily available by the time
you read this. The narrative is based on the Commodore 64
version only, since other versions were not available at this
writing. However, experience assures that they will be
substantially the same. If there are loading differences in the
IBM *Scenery Disk,* substitute its instructions for the loading
instructions below.

Boot your *Flight Simulator* disk in the usual way and enter the editor. With the *Flight Simulator* disk still in the drive, type in the following parameters:

North Position: 12795
East Position: 14102
Altitude: 0
Pitch: 0
Bank: 0
Heading: 45
Airspeed: 0
Throttle: 0

Rudder: 32767
Ailerons: 32767
Flaps: 0
Elevators: 32767
Time: 15:00
Season: 2—Spring
Wind: 3 Kts, 68

Exit the editor. Replace the *Flight Simulator* disk with *Scenery Disk 1*. Hold down CTRL and press E. You'll get a Current Databases listing. Press any key. There'll be a disk access and you'll find yourself just off runway 6 at East Texas Regional Airport, Nacogdoches, Texas. Get out your Houston sectional chart (the one that came with *Scenery Disk 1)* and locate airport 4 near the center. That's where you are.

Nacogdoches is a historic town, home in the 1800s to the Indian tribe of the same name. The first oil well drilled in Texas was drilled here in 1866.

Go into radar and zoom up until the runways disappear, and you see two towns connected by a highway and a bit of water that looks like the front end of a goose on the run. The town to the south is Lufkin, Texas, and the one ahead of you is Nacogdoches. The highway is U.S. 59. The body of water is Sam Rayburn Reservoir, named for the onetime Speaker of the House who represented Texas for 48 years.

Return to the out-the-windshield view and ready your aircraft for takeoff. We'll fly contact this afternoon—in other words, purely with reference to our sectional chart and the scenery below. Our cruise altitude will be 2300 feet.

Take off when you're ready, and maneuver to get over the reservoir on a heading of about 130, or whatever keeps the broadest expanse of water directly ahead of you.

After your flight has settled down, check radar and zoom to the view which shows you three large bodies of water. The one to your left is Toledo Bend Reservoir, on the Texas-Louisiana border. The one to the right is Lake Livingston, about 25 miles from Huntsville, Texas.

Correct your course as needed to follow the reservoir proper. Let the tranquility of earth, sky, and water, and the lazy drone of the engine, relax you. This is a very pretty vista.

To confirm that you're really a part of civilization, you might want to tune Lufkin VOR on 112.1. At least it'll put a reading on your DME, which reading, however, has little to do with the flight we're making.

Our destination, in case you were wondering, is a little strip a bit south of the southern end of the reservoir—Bell Field in Jasper County. It's airport 17 on your Houston sectional chart.

You might as well start staring hard at that chart. Because I'll have no further tips. I'm just along for the ride. You're certainly skilled enough, after all the flying we've done together, to put yourself down at Bell Field handily. And with bells on.

I'll expect a beautiful landing from you. The whole bit. Approach at approach speed and altitude. Forty-five degree entry into the pattern. Carburetor heat. Full flaps at the right time. Nice steady final. And grease it on.

As for me, I'll just sit back and admire the scenery.

This is the end now of 80 adventures in *Flight Simulator.* We've come a long way and been many places together. I've enjoyed every moment and every mile, and hope you have too.

Now I'm waiting anxiously for more of the *Scenery Disk*s, particularly the *Star Scenery Disk*s, which will feature smaller areas but significantly more detail.

And in particular, I'm anxiously watching for the new, upscale simulator Bruce Artwick is reportedly designing for the new Commodore Amiga computer. The job couldn't be in better hands. And with the Amiga's speed, color, and graphic prowess, that simulator should be something else.

When any or all of these developments are available, I'll be off, I'm sure, on more journeys. Maybe we can get together again then.

Meanwhile, thanks for your company. Enjoyed flying with you.

Appendix
Piper Area Charts

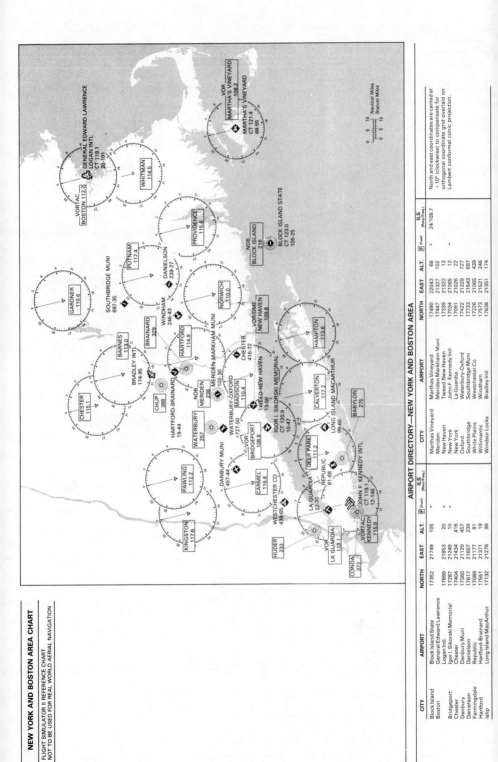

NEW YORK AND BOSTON AREA CHART

FLIGHT SIMULATOR II REFERENCE CHART
NOT TO BE USED FOR REAL WORLD AERIAL NAVIGATION

Reprinted courtesy of SubLogic Corporation. Copyright 1984.

SEATTLE AREA CHART

FLIGHT SIMULATOR II REFERENCE CHART. NOT TO BE USED FOR REAL WORLD AERIAL NAVIGATION

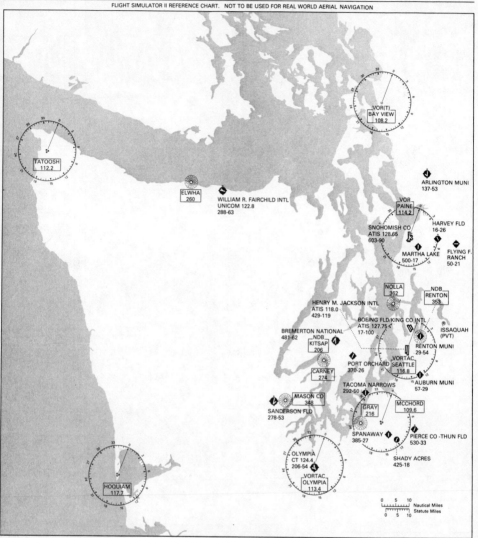

AIRPORT DIRECTORY—SEATTLE AREA

CITY	AIRPORT	NORTH	EAST	ALT.	F (Fuel)	ILS (Rwy/Freq.)
Alderwood Manor	Martha Lake	21502	6670	500		
Arlington	Arlington Muni	21616	6737	137		
Auburn	Auburn Muni	21290	6586	57		
Bremerton	Bremerton National	21407	6470	481		
Everett	Snohomish Co	21525	6665	603	*	16/109.3
Issaquah	Issaquah	21362	6668	500	*	
Monroe	Flying F. Ranch	21481	6738	50		
Olympia	Olympia	21218	6343	206	*	
Puyallup	Pierce Co.-Thun Fld	21206	6534	530		
Port Angeles	William R. Fairchild Intl.	21740	6375	288	*	
Port Orchard	Port Orchard	21373	6483	370		
Renton	Renton Muni	21351	6612	29		
Seattle	Boeing Fld/King Co Intl	21376	6596	17	*	
Seattle	Henry M. Jackson Intl. (Seattle-Tacoma Intl)	21343	6584	429		
Shelton	Sanderson Fld.	21353	6316	278		
Snohomish Co. (Paine Field) see Everett						
Snohomish	Harvey Fld	21505	6711	16		
Spanaway	Shady Acres	21201	6501	425		
Spanaway	Spanaway	21215	6491	385		
Tacoma	Tacoma Narrows	21300	6480	292		

North and east coordinates are canted at −21° (counterclockwise) to compensate for orthogonal coordinate grid overlaid on Lambert conformal conic projection.

LOS ANGELES AREA CHART

FLIGHT SIMULATOR II REFERENCE CHART. NOT TO BE USED FOR REAL WORLD AERIAL NAVIGATION

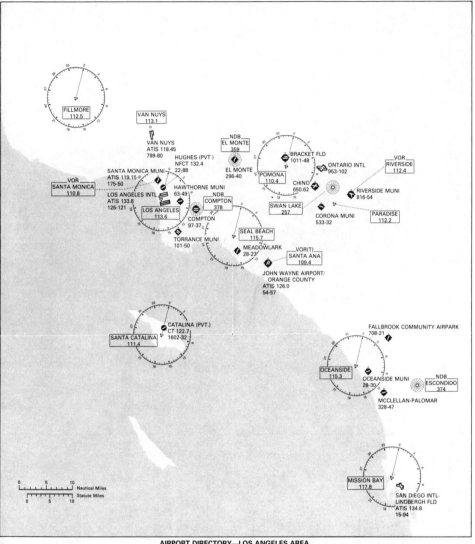

AIRPORT DIRECTORY—LOS ANGELES AREA

CITY	AIRPORT	NORTH	EAST	ALT.	F (Fuel)	ILS (Rwy/Freq.)
Carlsbad	McClennan-Palomar	14931	6112	328		
	Catalina (PVT)	15149	5744	1602		
Chino	Chino	15319	6079	650		
Compton	Compton	15,334	5859	97		
Corona	Corona Muni	15280	6083	533		
El Monte	El Monte	15397	5952	296		
Fallbrook	Fallbrook Community Airpark	15023	6144	708		
Hawthorne	Hawthorne Muni	15358	5831	63		
Huntington Beach	Meadowlark	15244	5911	28		
LaVerne	Brackett Fld	15378	6038	1011		
Los Angeles	Hughes (PVT)	15386	5808	22	*	
Los Angeles	Los Angeles Intl	15374	5805	126	*	
Oceanside	Oceanside Muni	14974	6095	28		
Ontario	Ontario Intl	15347	6099	952		
Riverside	Riverside Muni	15288	6141	816		
San Diego	San Diego Intl–Lingbergh Fld	14761	6102	15	*	
Santa Ana	John Wayne Airport/					
	Orange County	15211	5961	54		
Santa Monica	Santa Monica Muni	15402	5799	175	*	
Torrance	Torrance Muni	15308	5815	101		
Van Nuys	Van Nuys	15498	5811	799	*	16R/111.3

North and east coordinates are canted at −19° (counterclockwise) to compensate for orthogonal coordinate grid overlaid on Lambert conformal conic projection.

Reprinted courtesy of SubLogic Corporation. Copyright 1984.

AIRPORT DIRECTORY—CHICAGO AREA

CITY	AIRPORT	NORTH	EAST	ALT.	E (Fuel)	ILS (Rwy/Freq.)
Aurora	Aurora Muni	17152	16393	706		
Bloomington	Bloomington-Normal	16593	16246	875		
Champaign (Urbana)	University of Illinois Willard	16400	16465	754	*	31/109.1
Chicago	Chicago Midway	17156	16628	619	*	
Chicago	Chicago-O'Hare Intl	17243	16578	667	*	
Chicago	Lansing Muni	17049	16697	614		
Chicago	Merrill C. Meigs	17189	16671	592	*	
Chicago-Blue Island	Howel	17100	16627	600		
Chicago-Schaumburg	Schaumburg Air Park	17247	16515	795		
Chicago/West Chicago)	DuPage	17213	16466	757		
Danville	Vermilion Co	16471	16685	695		
Dwight	Dwight	16874	16404	630		
Frankfort	Frankfort	17025	16696	775		
Gibson City	Gibson City Muni	16594	16461	759		
Joliet	Joliet Park District	17038	16490	582		
Kankakee	Greater Kankakee	16846	16597	625	*	
Monee	Sanger	16980	16646	786		
Morris	Morris Muni	17004	16413	588		
New Lenox	New Lenox-Howell	17025	16571	745		
Paxton	Paxton	16578	16507	780		
Plainfield	Clow Intl	17116	16502	670		
Romeoville	Lewis University	17081	16518	672		
Urbana	Frasca Field	16448	16482	735		

North and east coordinates align with orthogonal coordinate grid overlaid on Lambert conformal conic projection.

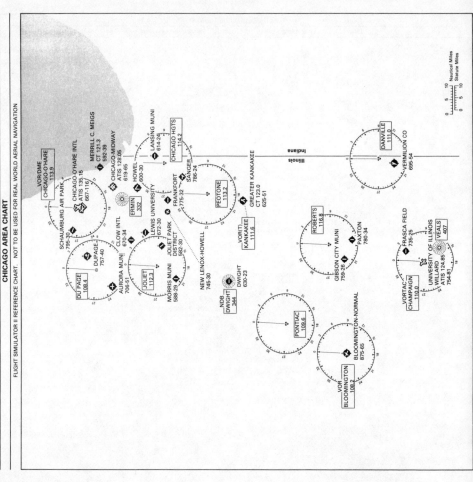

CHICAGO AREA CHART

FLIGHT SIMULATOR II REFERENCE CHART. NOT TO BE USED FOR REAL WORLD AERIAL NAVIGATION

LEGEND

☂ ◆ ● Civil-Public use airport

® Restricted/Private-Nonpublic use airport, having emergency use or landmark value

✿ Rotating light in operation, sunset to sunrise

SANTA MONICA
ATIS 119.15
175-50
Airport Name
Advisory Frequency (if available)
Elevation (feet) — Length (hundreds of feet)

NAME
FREQUENCY   VOR

NAME
FREQUENCY   VORTAC (Distance Measuring Equipment Able)

NAME
FREQUENCY   VOR/DME

NAME
FREQUENCY   Non Directional Beacon

VOR/DME
NAME
FREQUENCY
If VOR falls directly on an airport, only the airport symbol will be shown. The VOR facility type is shown at the top of the box.

AIRPORT NAME ABBREVIATIONS
CO   County
FLD   Field
INTL   International
MUNI   Municipal
(PVT)   Private Airport (prior permission before landing)

Reprinted courtesy of SubLogic Corporation. Copyright 1984

If you've enjoyed the articles in this book, you'll find the same style and quality in every monthly issue of **COMPUTE!** Magazine. Use this form to order your subscription to **COMPUTE!**.

For Fastest Service
Call Our **Toll-Free** US Order Line
1-800-247-5470
In IA call 1-800-532-1272

COMPUTE!
P.O. Box 10954
Des Moines, IA 50340

My computer is:
☐ Commodore 64 or 128 ☐ TI-99/4A ☐ IBM PC or PCjr ☐ VIC-20
☐ Apple ☐ Atari ☐ Amiga ☐ Other _____
☐ Don't yet have one...

☐ $24 One Year US Subscription
☐ $45 Two Year US Subscription
☐ $65 Three Year US Subscription
Subscription rates outside the US:
☐ $30 Canada and Foreign Surface Mail
☐ $65 Foreign Air Delivery

Name _____

Address _____

City _____ State _____ Zip _____

Country _____

Payment must be in US funds drawn on a US bank, international money order, or charge card.
☐ Payment Enclosed ☐ Visa
☐ MasterCard ☐ American Express

Acct. No. _____ Expires _____ / _____
(Required)

Your subscription will begin with the next available issue. Please allow 4–6 weeks for delivery of first issue. Subscription prices subject to change at any time.

46419333

COMPUTE! Books

Ask your retailer for these **COMPUTE! Books** or order directly from **COMPUTE!**.

Call toll free (in US) **1-800-346-6767** (in NY 212-887-8525) or write COMPUTE! Books, P.O. Box 5038, F.D.R. Station, New York, NY 10150.

Quantity	Title	Price*	Total
_____	Becoming a MacArtist (80-9)	**$17.95**	_____
_____	COMPUTE!'s Apple Games for Kids (91-4)	**$12.95**	_____
_____	COMPUTE!'s First Book of Apple (69-8)	**$12.95**	_____
_____	COMPUTE!'s Guide to Telecomputing on the Apple (98-1)	**$ 9.95**	_____
_____	COMPUTE!'s Kids and the Apple (76-0)	**$12.95**	_____
_____	Easy BASIC Programs for the Apple (88-4)	**$14.95**	_____
_____	MacTalk: Telecomputing on the Macintosh (85-X)	**$14.95**	_____
_____	SpeedScript: The Word Processor for Apple Personal Computers (000)	**$ 9.95**	_____
_____	The Apple IIc: Your First Computer (001)	**$ 9.95**	_____
_____	Apple Machine Language for Beginners (002)	**$14.95**	_____
_____	COMPUTE!'s Second Book of Apple (008)	**$12.95**	_____
_____	MacOffice: Using the Macintosh for Everything (006)	**$14.95**	_____
_____	MacIdeas (015-7)	**$14.95**	_____
_____	Using Your Macintosh: Beginning Microsoft BASIC and Applications (021-1)	**$16.95**	_____
_____	Apple II Applications: 40 Programs for Your Apple (016-5)	**$14.95**	_____
_____	Advanced Macintosh BASIC Programming (030-0)	**$16.95**	_____
_____	COMPUTE!'s Third Book of Apple (063-7)	**$14.95**	_____

*Add $2.00 per book for shipping and handling.
Outside US add $5.00 air mail or $2.00 surface mail.

NC residents add 4.5% sales tax. _____
NY residents add 8.25% sales tax _____
Shipping & handling: $2.00/book _____
Total payment _____

All orders must be prepaid (check, charge, or money order).
All payments must be in US funds.
☐ Payment enclosed.
Charge   ☐ Visa   ☐ MasterCard   ☐ American Express

Acct. No. _____ Exp. Date _____
(Required)

Name _____

Address _____

City _____ State _____ Zip _____

*Allow 4–5 weeks for delivery.
Prices and availability subject to change.
Current catalog available upon request.

46404313